2

VICTORIAN PEOPLE

LONDON, 1872
An engraving by Gustave Doré of Ludgate Hill

VICTORIAN PEOPLE

In life and in literature

GILLIAN AVERY

HOLT, RINEHART AND WINSTON, INC.

New York · Chicago · San Francisco

books by Gillian Avery

CALL OF THE VALLEY

SBN: 03–066655–4 (Trade)
SBN: 03–066660–0 (HLE)

Library of Congress Catalog Card Number: 76–98927

Printed in Great Britain

First Edition

Contents

Author's Note

In the following pages there are frequent references to the cost of articles and to wages in the Victorian period. It is of course impossible to translate these into terms of modern money, and even an attempt to show the purchasing power of an equivalent modern sum can be very confusing, since prices fluctuated unevenly. Many prices dropped heavily as the century progressed and more economical methods of industrial production were introduced. Thus *The Times* newspaper (which in 1970 costs eightpence) was fivepence in early Victorian days and only one penny in 1916. Recipients of a letter parcel in 1837 would have to pay a couple of shillings for the postage; with the introduction of Penny Postage in 1840 a letter could be sent for one penny (four‑pence or fivepence in 1970, according to how fast one wants it to travel). An early Victorian three volume novel might cost thirty shillings (three weeks' wages for an agricultural labourer of the time), but by the end of the century cheap editions of popular classics could be bought for sevenpence (as against five shillings in 1970 for a paperback novel). Up to the end of the century it was perfectly possible to live in lower middle class comfort for under £100 a year, and my husband's grandfather, a Lancashire schoolmaster, started his married life in 1895 on £70 a year from which he managed to save a little every year. (His 1970 equivalent would be earning rather more than ten times as much.) On page 94 we see how an Oxfordshire woman laid out the twelve weekly shillings that her husband earned in 1869; a 1970 advertisement for a cowman in Oxfordshire offers £20 a week.

1 · *Victorian Times*

QUEEN VICTORIA reigned for sixty-three years, the longest reign in English history. At the end of the century a man or woman who remembered her accession in 1837 would have seen her change from a headstrong, wilful girl of 18, of whom many disapproved, into a venerable old woman who seemed to symbolize the dignity and the authority of the British Empire. And the realm that she ruled changed as much as she did. From the 1830's, crippled by the effects of the Napoleonic Wars, seething with discontent, it moved to the calm and prosperity of the late decades of the century; proud in the contemplation of the peaceful years that lay behind, in the far-flung possessions of the British Empire overseas; proud of the British way of life and the British rule.

The villagers at Lark Rise, that Oxfordshire hamlet to which reference will be made in chapters to come, did not awake to the benefits that the reign of Victoria had conferred on them until the year of her Golden Jubilee in 1887. Up to then they had hardly thought of their Queen except as a cross old woman who was supposed to have shut herself up in Balmoral Castle and refused to come to London to open Parliament when Mr. Gladstone begged her to. But in the June of 1887 they became enthusiastic. "Fancy her reigning fifty years, the old dear, her!" they said, and bought paper banners inscribed *Fifty Years, Mother, Wife, and Queen*, to put inside their windows, or jam jars inscribed *1837 to 1887. Victoria the Good*, and

From the title page of *The Children's Friend*, 1866.

7

"THE QUEEN OF EARTHLY QUEENS"

Queen Victoria arrives at St. Paul's Cathedral on 22 June 1897, for a service of thanksgiving to mark her Diamond Jubilee, accompanied by a procession whose splendour, said *The Times,* had "never been paralleled in the history of the world." Painting by A. C. Gow in the Guildhall Art Gallery, London.

Radio Times Hulton Picture Library

below this *Peace and Plenty*. The newspapers told them how much had
been achieved in her reign: railway travel; the telegraph; Free Trade;
exports; progress; prosperity; Peace. All, it seemed, due to her inspiration.
And with loyal zeal, every woman in the hamlet produced her penny,
polished and wrapped in a piece of tissue paper, to subscribe to the Jubilee
present which the women of England were making to the Queen.

The Victorians were proud of the peace, progress and prosperity of their era, which they felt was unparallelled in English history. Certainly it would be difficult to find years so unbroken by war. The battle of Waterloo in 1815 had ended not only over twenty years of French wars, but also a century and more of intermittent struggle with France. England settled down then to lick her wounds, and the peace was not broken until the Crimean War of 1854–6, when she found herself allied with France[1] and fighting the Russians in (so far as the English were concerned) a somewhat pointless imbroglio over Russian power in the Middle East. It was a war fought far from home, and not much was felt to be at stake, though the incompetence of the generals (who after four decades of peace were quite without experience of active service) and the hopeless muddles of the civil administration whipped the British public into a frenzy of indignation.

In the years that followed there was more interest in military affairs. Britain had been shaken by the Crimean War and set to work to reform her army. She watched uneasily, too, the wars on the Continent and the Civil War in America. There were various troubles of her own to deal with in the far-flung possessions of the British Empire: the Indian Mutiny of 1857, the Afghan War of 1878; disturbances in British-administered territories of Africa, culminating in the South African War of 1898. For all these strong armed forces were needed, but Britain was involved in no European war until 1914.

When the Victorians spoke proudly of the progress of the past sixty years, they meant not only material achievements – the development of trade and industry, symbolized by the Great Exhibition of 1851, the bridges built, the railways laid, the civic buildings, the hospitals, the drainage, the schools. They meant the energy they had brought into reforming the civil service, the army, municipal administration, prisons; the education system that they had established, the new life they had breathed into the church. They were proud of the new decency and respectability that they had introduced into private and public life after the loud coarse ways and the brutality and corruption of the previous generation. And they gloried in the British possessions scattered in every continent and every ocean,

1 The habit of regarding the French as the enemy died hard. Lord Raglan, the commander of the British forces in the Crimea, used absentmindedly to refer to his opponents as "the French", forgetting that this time they were supposed to be friends.

LONDON THRONGS TO THE GREAT EXHIBITION

This first international display of industrial products, promoted by Prince Albert, marked the emergence of Britain from the hungry forties into an age of prosperity. The drawing by Cruikshank shows Piccadilly jammed with traffic on its way to Hyde Park to visit the Exhibition in the Crystal Palace.

Radio Times Hulton Picture Library

men of thousands of languages and dialects, hundreds of races, all owing allegiance to the British Crown; nearly a quarter of the world, and a quarter of the world population – the Empire on which the sun never set.

The early Victorians had found England in a chaotic state of hunger and near-revolution. Industrialism was creeping over the land. It had been clouding the air since the end of the century, but with the distractions and the demands of the French wars, it had been largely ignored. England's days as a predominantly agricultural country were over; it was for the Victorians to organize the urban civilization that took its place.

Up to the early decades of the 19th century England's economy, administration and government had rested on the assumption that it was agriculture that mattered and had to be supported at all costs. The English land-owners were the ruling men, it was their interests that were considered. They voted themselves into Parliament, they made the laws. The English farmer was protected by the Corn Laws from competition with cheaper, imported foodstuffs. The Corn Laws, introduced in 1815, forbade the import of foreign corn when the price of English corn was under a certain price, and were later amended so that the duty payable on imported corn varied according to the price of corn at home. When English corn was relatively cheap then the import duty on foreign corn was high. The poor who could not afford the price of bread were often brought to desperate straits, but those who made the laws insisted that the country's economy

ELECTRICITY – WHAT WILL HE GROW TO?
Punch in a cartoon of 1881 shows King Steam and King Coal contemplating the infant Electricity. Improved methods for the storage of electrical force had recently been discovered.

would collapse unless her agriculture was propped up, and then where would the poor be?

It was not until 1846 that the Corn Laws were repealed, after years of bitterness and clamour and violent protests from the manufacturers. The manufacturers, who by this time were an increasingly powerful body, maintained that as long as Britain refused to import foreign grain except at a high rate of duty, foreign buyers would retaliate by refusing to buy British manufactures. The warehouses of Lancashire were piled high with cotton goods that could not be sold; in the Potteries and the Black Country and the cloth towns of the west men could find no employment and were starving because of the price of bread. "I have no hesitation in saying," Gladstone[1] was reported to have said, "that if the repeal of the Corn Laws had been defeated or even retarded, we should have had a revolution." And so in 1846 Britain moved from Protection to Free Trade. Free Trade – ports open without restriction to imports and exports – was to remain until in the 1880's the new theories of imperialism and tariff reform began to create a different climate of opinion.

In those years before the repeal of the Corn Laws – the "hungry forties" they were called – the spectre of revolution haunted responsible men. England seemed to be shivering on the edge of an abyss. Working men urged revolution at political meetings; foreign visitors such as de Tocqueville weighed up the probabilities; starving labourers set fire to farmers' ricks; there were clashes with the military. One agitator for Free Trade and the abolition of the Corn Laws forecast a repetition of the French rising of 1830; another threatened the young Queen with the fate of Louis XVI.

These were the years of the Chartists. No one knew the strength of the Chartist movement or its powers of organization. It was a hidden force, the thought of which terrified people by its supposed designs. The Charter of the Chartists was a document accepted in 1838 by a variety of working men's groups who agreed that they should sink their own separate agitations into agitation for a common cause. They hoped by parliamentary reform to alleviate the hopeless conditions in which they lived and laboured. They demanded a vote for every man of the population, annual parlia

1 William Ewart Gladstone, 1809–1898. Liberal Prime Minister first in 1868. One of the greatest British parliamentarians and orators, he and his great political opponent, Disraeli, dominated English politics during the second half of the century.

ments, payment of the members, secret ballots, equal electoral districts, and the removal of property qualifications for members of Parliament. These points gained, working men could vote themselves into Parliament and make laws that would provide bread for their starving children. Or so they told themselves.

Support for the Chartists varied from year to year. When conditions were particularly bad then the workers' passions rose, but as soon as things improved their interest waned. And though the movement produced much violent talk there was in fact little real violence. Twice the Charter was presented to Parliament and rejected. The third and final occasion was in 1848. Panic swept the country when the Chartist leader Feargus O'Connor announced that half a million people would meet on Kennington Common and march to Westminster with a petition containing seven million signatures. Britain seemed to be caught up in the storm which had already whirled over half Europe, and had swept away rulers and governments. Troops were posted along the route, special constables were enrolled.

But only a small proportion of the demonstrators ever met at Kennington, and the presence of the police, a general apathy, and heavy rain deterred those that did. The march was never made, a vast number of the seven million signatures were found to be false. Chartism was dead, the revolution was over. But the reforms that the Chartists demanded were for the most part achieved in the next forty years, and in 1885 there was a working man sitting in the House of Commons as a Liberal M.P.; Joseph Arch, who had spent forty years of his life as an agricultural labourer.

A beginning had been made in 1832, with the great Reform Act. Before 1832 Parliament had in no way represented the interests of the great majority of the population. It had represented the interests of the wealthy landowner, who probably sat in the House of Lords himself and saw to it that the House of Commons was filled with his creatures. To be able to vote at all was a privilege only allowed to property owners with a certain income. Candidates were able to bribe the electors (who had to declare their votes publicly and aloud), seats in the House of Commons could be bought and sold like houses, and many of the new industrial towns, such as Manchester, were not represented at all. Landowners had in many cases the absolute right to nominate a member of Parliament (in such cases the constituencies were known as "nomination boroughs" and

UP FROM THE COUNTRY – 1851

Farm workers and their families marvel at the splendours of the Great Exhibition.

(Illustrated London News)

Radio Times Hulton Picture Library

might have no inhabitants at all, or even, as in the case of Dunwich, have disappeared under the sea.)

The 1832 Reform Act by no means stripped the power of the landowners. But a wedge was driven under the feet of the great aristocratic Colossus that bestraddled the country; it began, very slightly, to topple. As the century progressed succeeding reform acts gave voting powers to more and more of the population, until in 1884 all men over the age of 21 were eligible. Voting by this time had become secret and the bribing of electors illegal.

By 1884 the working man had thus achieved a say in the affairs of his country. His life too was becoming more tolerable, he was better housed, assured of an elementary education, provided with more amenities for his leisure. Working conditions in factories had improved, trade unions were recognized as legal. For all this the Victorians had provided legislation.

It was not just a matter of making laws and seeing that they were applied; reformers had also to fight the general feeling that all this was outrageous interference with the liberty of the individual, who had a right to keep piles of manure in the streets, or leave his factory machinery unfenced even if his workers fell into it. Patiently, diligently, the reformers of the 30's and 40's sought to bring some sort of order into the chaos of those early years of the factory age. They scrutinized, probed, catechized, and then prepared their reports and statistics. No community in history, G. M. Young remarked,[1] had ever been submitted to so searching an examination. Industrial and living conditions were investigated by Parliamentary Committees and Royal Commissions, and their findings issued to the public in Parliamentary Blue Books. Among them were such famous reports as the Employment of Children Enquiry of 1840, which described and illustrated the horrifying work which small children were undertaking in mines, and led to the Coal Mines Act two years later, forbidding the employment of women and children underground. In 1842 the enquiry led by Sir Edwin Chadwick published its report on the Sanitary Conditions of the Labouring Classes, a grim account of the bestial conditions in which thousands were living.

But it was a long time before the progress which had made the middle classes more respectable and more comfortable did the same for the workers. It was one thing to present the hideous facts of the lives of the labouring poor to the public, another to provide legislation to improve this, and yet another to see that it was carried into effect when there was as yet no proper organization, and no competent municipal authorities. All this still remained to be provided – but long before the end of the century it was achieved, and though horrifying tracts of slums still remained in the cities, at least they were recognized as slums, instead of being accepted as the normal place for the poor to live.

The factory age had since the closing years of the old century already done much to alter the traditional pattern of English life. The coming of the railways further disrupted it. The railways changed the face of England. Ancient towns which refused to accept them were left in sleepy oblivion to shrink and lose their importance, while the population of rivals soared. Cities such as London and Birmingham became ringed with suburbs where the more prosperous, with the advent of a relatively cheap form of transport, were now able to live. A school like Manchester Grammar School no longer drew its pupils just from the neighbourhood, but from

1 G. M. Young: *Portrait of an Age,* 1936.

THE RAILWAY—FIRST CLASS.

SECOND CLASS.

THIRD CLASS.

Railways in 1847 provided three types of accomodation.

From *The Illustrated London News*

many parts of Lancashire, Cheshire, even Yorkshire. Before the railways the movement of people was limited to the distance a horse could travel. With railways even a city clerk could live miles from his work. New towns sprang up outside the big cities; seaside towns and watering places became important as people who had hitherto passed their lives within a small radius of their homes now began to insist on holidays with sea-bathing or "cures" – luxuries which an earlier generation had not contemplated.

As early as 1825 George Stephenson had driven at a speed of 12 miles an hour in a steam locomotive along the Stockton to Darlington railway. But it was not until 1830 when the Liverpool to Manchester railway was opened that rail communications really got under way. The '30's and the '40's were the years of the rail mania. With colossal, undaunted energy the early Victorians set to work to cover England with a maze of railway lines, blasting out tunnels, raising up embankments, digging away cut-tings, spanning valleys with viaducts, permanently altering the English landscape with their picks, spades and wheelbarrows – for more elaborate engineering apparatus was hardly available then. Gangs of labourers, many of them Irish, to whom the name "navvy"[1] was given – lived in camps with their families, shaping the railways which were beginning to wind their way all over the countryside. The 20th century was to inherit a mass of routes that often duplicated each other, and became superfluous when railways were nationalized and were no longer run by a host of competing private companies. The canals with which the late 18th century had thought to revolutionize England's transport fell into disuse, or were bought up by the companies so that they might be abandoned. The mail coach service, at the height of its efficiency in the early years of the century, went out of business; so did many of the coaching inns along the roads. Thousands of people thought that their fortunes were going to be made in the railways, and rushed to sink their capital in the latest company to put out its optimistic prospectus. Some fortunes were made, but many others were lost through rash speculation. Particularly unfortunate were those investors putting their trust in George Hudson, the "Railway King", who soared into high society, even to the extent of friendship with the Prince Consort, in the 1840's, only to crash to ruin in 1854, with a loss to the investors, it was estimated, of £80,000,000.

1 The men who had dug out the canals of late 18th century England had been called navigators; navvy was an abbreviation of this.

THE RAILWAY JUGGERNAUT OF 1845

Punch shows a frenzied mob rushing to throw themselves under the wheels of an advancing locomotive, and comments: "The year was indeed signalized by the earlier signs of that outbreak of feverish speculation which was known as the 'Railway Mania'".

The energy and the passion that the early Victorians brought to such matters as railways and reform, they also brought to intellectual affairs. It was the age of great tumult within the Anglican Church, when the Tractarians sought to remind it of its divine origins and to turn its face towards those early centuries when the Christian Church had been undivided. In 1845 Newman,[1] now convinced that the infallible church that he sought could not be found within the Anglican Church, left it to join the Church of Rome, taking with him a host of others – clergy and laymen. Those were stormy, unhappy years for the English church, when

[1] John Henry Newman, 1801–90. Founded 1833 with Keble, Pusey, and R. H. Froude, all of them Oxford academics, the Oxford Movement, known also as the Tractarian movement. Created cardinal of the Roman Catholic Church in 1879. One of the most distinguished theologians and writers of the century.

feelings on religious differences were passionate, even violent, when families were split apart, and men lost their friends.

Profound interest in religious matters persisted throughout the 19th century. The early Victorians had felt they were taking part in a religious revival, and their doubts had turned upon what form their religion should take. Later Victorians questioned more fundamental matters, they questioned the very nature of religious belief. Religious doubt was in the air. Darwin's *Origin of Species*, published in 1859, was held by many to have struck a fatal blow at the church's traditional teaching on the origin of human life; German theologians were destroying belief in the literal truth of the Bible.

Victorian intellectual energy produced a great literature, and a public who enjoyed it. There was curious unanimity in men's tastes. The working man venerated Tennyson, and the intellectuals no less so. Dickens' novels were read by all classes with an eagerness that could hardly contain itself between instalments. As each monthly number appeared it was read aloud to the gathered family in thousands of homes. The Victorian period produced novelists worthy of their times, capable – more so than at any other epoch – of scrutinizing and commenting on the changing pattern of society and ideas. Victorians seen through the eyes of Victorians – the following chapters will try to illustrate the use that such novelists as Dickens, George Eliot, and Trollope made of the times they lived in.

Of these changing times the villagers of Lark Rise were little aware. An agricultural community is a conservative one, slow and reluctant to change. Lark Rise was grateful for peace, prosperity and progress because the newspapers told them they should be. "Peace? Of course there was peace. War was something you read about in books, something rather exciting, if only the poor soldiers had not to be killed, but all long ago and far away, something that could not possibly happen in our time." Progress? They saw little of that. Railways were far away and few of them had seen one, though bicycles had appeared and were thought to be dangerous and frightening, and the penny postage sometimes brought them a letter from sons or daughters gone away to work. Prosperity belonged to others, to the town dweller who was becoming enriched at the expense of those who worked on the land. But they all agreed that Victoria was a good Queen, and when asked why would reply, "Because she's brought the price of the quartern loaf down," or "Well, we have got peace under her, haven't we?"

But in Lark Rise after that Jubilee year of 1887 nothing ever seemed quite the same. The farmer who employed nearly all the inhabitants intro/duced a new self/binding reaping machine so that women were no longer needed to help in the harvest field. The new Rector's wife took the mem/bers of her Mothers' Meeting for an expedition to London by train. The innkeeper's wife got in cases of tinned salmon and Australian rabbit. The Sanitary Inspector came to the hamlet for the first time and disapproved of what he saw there. Wages rose, so did prices, people suddenly realized that they needed things that they had never before thought to possess. And they began to speak of "before the Jubilee" as a generation now speaks of "before the war" – either as a golden time, or as one of exploded ideas. The town life that the Victorian period had brought to the rest of England had reached Lark Rise.

(*Illustrated London News,* 1845)

2 · French and American Visitors

VISITORS from abroad inspected Victorian England with much curiosity; it seemed so strange and so foreign. They wanted to see the industry and the railways quite as much as they wanted to study its history and inspect its ancient monuments. People came to marvel at the factories and report on the effect industrial conditions had upon the population. But when we read their appalled comments we must remember that they were seeing this sort of misery for the first time – the product of a new urban civilization which nobody had yet learned how to handle. They were also seeing it against a background of rain and fog which as one of them, Taine, admitted, intensified the depression and gloom. Sun and warmth such as an Italian peasant might enjoy did much to soften poverty and make its aspect less ugly.

The best known of the foreign commentators on the Victorian scene are the French and the Americans. Of these the French were the politer and the better-disposed. The Americans were riled by English criticism of American manners so general at that time (they were justifiably inflamed

A traveller in a London cab. Drawing by Gustave Doré.

by Mrs. Frances Trollope's[1] *Domestic Manners of the Americans*, published in 1832, a shrewish piece of work, and by Dickens' *American Notes*, published in 1842 and his account of American ways in *Martin Chuzzlewit* a year later). This was particularly true of Nathaniel Hawthorne who spent four years in England as American Consul in Liverpool, where he saw the worst aspects of industrial England rather than the fair spreading lawns, the stately country houses, and the ancient towns that the ordinary visitor from abroad would have been led to admire.

All the visitors were struck by the huge gulf that existed between rich and poor, and all of them were led to comment on the English aristocracy,

THE BRITISH PASSION FOR INEQUALITY

Sturdy Briton. "It's all very well to turn up you nose at *your own* beggarly Counts and Barons, Mossoo. But you can't find fault with *our* nobility! Take a man like our Dook o' Bayswater, now! Why, he could buy up your foreign Dukes and Princes by the dozen! and as for you and me, he'd look upon us as so much dirt beneath his feet! Now, that's something *like* a nobleman, *that* is! That's a kind o' nobleman that I, as an Englishman, feel as I've got some right to be *proud* of!"

From *Mr Punch in Society*

1 Mrs. Frances Trollope (1780–1863), novelist, mother of Anthony Trollope.

the Americans because it was a phenomenon that did not exist in the States; the French because of the way the English aristocracy differed from their own. "These English are strangely proud of having a class above," observed Hawthorne, having marked a crowd of people staring reverently at Lord Derby's coach and four. And Elizabeth Davies Bancroft, the wife of the American Minister to England in the latter half of the 1840's complained how complex the class system was in the servants' hall. "I cannot make one of them do anything, except by the person and at the time which English custom prescribes. They are brought up to fill certain situations, and fill them perfectly, but cannot or will not vary.

Then she goes on to particularise:

"A lady's maid is a *very great* character *indeed*, and would be much more unwilling to take her tea with, or speak familiarly to, a footman or a house‑maid than I should. My greatest mistakes in England have been com‑mitted towards those high dignitaries, my own maid and the butler, whose grandeur I entirely misappreciated and invaded, as in my ignorance I

FASHIONABLE SERVANTS

Punch notes the practice among servants of referring to each other by their masters' rank.

Shopman: "Here! Hi! Are you his Grace the Duke of Bayswater?"

Magnificent Flunkey: "I ham!"

placed them, as we do, on the same level with other servants. She has her fire made for her, and *loaf* sugar in her tea, which she and Cates [the butler] sip in solitary majesty."

"They are brought up to fill certain situations," Mrs. Bancroft remarked, "but cannot or will not vary." This was not only a feature of the servants' halls, but applied to a large section of Victorian society. The really poor classes, as most of the foreign visitors were quick to point out, stood little chance of moving upwards, nor was it considered desirable that they they should attempt to do so. "The whole of English society is based upon privileges of money," said de Tocqueville. A man had to be rich to be a member of Parliament, a politician, a magistrate, a lawyer, a clergyman, or to go to law. There was not a country in the world where justice was more the privilege of the rich. Without money, intelligence and virtue were of little account. "The English have left the poor but two rights: that of obeying the same laws as the rich, and that of standing on an equality with them if they can obtain equal wealth. But these two rights are more apparent than real, since it is the rich who make the laws and who create for their own or their children's profit, the chief means of getting wealth."

Of all the observers who gazed at 19th century England Alexis de Tocqueville[1] had perhaps the most insight and understanding. He visited the country first in 1833 at a time when it seemed to many to be perilously near revolution. He was an unknown young magistrate then, fresh from the visit to America which was to result in *Democracy in America*. He stayed in England for five weeks on that occasion, visited the house of Commons, attended election meetings and a magistrates' court, and met influential political figures to whom he brought letters of introduction. He came to England, he told a friend in a letter, not to collect material for a new work, but rather to give himself "the intellectual pleasure of watching a great people in the throes of revolutionary change." It had been infinitely easier to formulate views about America than about England where "the roads cross, and you have to follow along each one of them to get a clear idea of the whole."

When he summed up his impressions of England after his first visit, he said that the state of the poor was England's deepest trouble, and that the

1 Alexis de Tocqueville (1805–1859), French statesman and writer.

A LONDON FOG

Fogs such as these were commonplace in cities such as London, Manchester and Liverpool, and appalled visiting foreigners. From *The Illustrated London News,* 1847.

cause of the evil was the way that landed property was divided up. "The English are still imbued with that doctrine . . . that great properties are necessary for the improvement of agriculture, and they still seem convinced that extreme inequality of wealth is the natural order of things." The country's danger lay in the conduct of the aristocracy, who, he feared, might try to oppose the current of new ideas, and who would be supported in this by the lesser landowners in a head-on clash with the workers and the new middle-class manufacturers.

But in spite of everything he was optimistic. "If things follow their natural course," he wrote, "I don't think there will be a revolution, and I see a good chance for the English to succeed in modifying the social and political set-up, with sharp growing pains, no doubt, but without convulsions, and without civil war."

When the American C. Edwards Lester visited England in 1839, he saw it in much the same state as it had been in 1835 at the time of de Tocqueville's second visit. He recorded his impressions in *The Glory and Shame of England* (1841). He was delighted with the scenery, astonished by the railways – the railway age was then beginning – and the enormous wealth expended on them. They were superior to the American ones, he thought, in "safety, speed, beauty, and durability."

He admired the domesticity of the English middle classes. "An English-man takes a bath in the morning; walks with his children in the garden; eats leisurely his cheerful breakfast; learns all the news; goes to his business and works hard till four o'clock, and then his work for the day is over. He spends a full hour at his dinner table; rides a few miles with his wife and children; and devotes the evening to society. He is satisfied if he is slowly accumulating; takes life easy, and enjoys himself as he goes along." He contrasts this easy-going life with American hustle. "Of how many Americans can it be said, they started on nothing – worked hard – got suddenly rich – became dyspeptic – just got ready to enjoy life – lost their fortune by speculation, or – were blown up in a steam-boat."

But he was horrified at the abysses of poverty he saw in England, and the economic distress. He went up to Lancashire, and found a starving popu-lation with the mills working short time. In Nottingham there were 3,000 people wandering round the streets with no work. The wool-spinning in Leicester was at a standstill, there was rick-firing by starving labourers in Devon. He marvelled at the English sympathy for "West Indian slaves, and Polish patriots, and heathen errors," while they could do nothing for the poor of their own country.

"I have seen more magnificence than I ever wish to see in my own country, and more wretchedness than I ever supposed could exist." The degradation of the poor he insisted was due to the miserably inadequate wage paid to the working man, which was further lowered by "a cruel bread-tax which takes food from their mouths to swell the incomes of the land-owners; or by poor-rates to feed the millions who have been made paupers by this very taxation system."

The iniquity of the Corn Laws, indeed, was the theme of his book. As an American he was naturally anxious that trade barriers should come down and that England should be free to import American grain and cotton, and genuinely grieved by the misery that the high price of bread caused among the poor: "The little, shivering, street-abandoned wretch that gets his loaf by selling small-ware, is robbed of the half of it to put diamonds in your shoe-buckles."

LONDON BEGGARS
An engraving by the French illustrator, Gustave Doré, from *London, A Pilgrimage,*
1872.

When the distinguished American historian William Hickling
Prescott visited England in 1850 he came as an honoured guest, and was
entertained by some of the greatest aristocrats in the country. He wrote home
warmly of their kindness and hospitality and made little comment on
those things that might not have pleased him so well, nor did he feel obliged
to look below the surface of the wealth and splendour that surrounded
him. But indeed matters had improved since Lester's visit; the Corn Laws
had been repealed, the "hungry forties" were over, England's trade was
on its feet again, its agriculture approaching a golden age of prosperity.

Prescott, far from being antagonized by the feudal state in which a great
landowner lived in England, found it pleasing. "They are extremely
beloved by their large tenantry," he wrote enthusiastically during a visit
to the Duke and Duchess of Northumberland at Alnwick Castle, and

reported that the Duke was devoted to the interests of those who lived on his estates, to their education and their comfort. He and his wife visited the poor cottages constantly, and the latter even helped with the teaching in the school she had established. "One of the prettiest sights was the assembly of these children in one of the Castle courts, making their processions in the order of their schools; that of the Duchess being distinguished by green jackets. The Duke and Duchess stood on the steps, and the little children, as they passed, all made their bows and courtesies, a band playing all the while."

Of the aristocracy as a class, Prescott observed – as others were to observe – that there perhaps never had been a nobility who took their responsibilities so seriously, and so little abused their great advantages. They were deeply conscientious, religious, zealous in improving their estates, and attentive to the needs of those who lived on them.

His most unfavourable remarks were reserved for the weather. He alleged that in England it rained twice as much as in America, and in the North

THE AMERICAN VISITOR IN OXFORD

Mr. Jonah P. Skeggs, from Chicago (with his family) suddenly bursts in on Jones, who has his rooms at Letter A, in the Cloisters.

Sir – we offer you – many apologies – for this – unwarrantable intrusion! We were not aware the old ruin was inhabited!

Du Maurier drawing from *Punch,* 1893

and in Scotland four times as much. He wondered that the ladies did not grow web-footed, since they seemed to pay no attention to the weather. He noted, too, the filth of London with its funeral pall of smoke, which made the outside of the buildings black as a chimney, and discoloured everything within. But he followed up this remark with a comment on the gay scenes in the streets in the fashionable area where he was staying. "Splendid equipages fill the great streets as far as the eye can reach, blazing with rich colours, and silver mountings, and gaudy liveries. Everything here tells of a proud and rich aristocracy."

But in spite of this; in spite of the princely state which the Duke and Duchess of Northumberland lived at Alnwick, and their grateful and devoted tenantry, and the lavish splendour with which the Earl of Carlisle entertained the Queen and her court at Castle Howard, Prescott could detect that the day of the aristocracy was passing, that the manufacturers and the men of money were succeeding to their place. Half jokingly he attributed their decline to the coming of the railways and the general level-ling brought about by a form of transport used by all sections of the com-munity.

Nathaniel Hawthorne's[1] feelings about England were not so cordial as Prescott's. He was not a feted guest, he was employed there in not specially congenial work, and in Liverpool he experienced not only the worst of England's weather, but witnessed the mid-century English industrial city at its most squalid and depressing. And perhaps more than any of the other American visitors he was irked by the continual quizzing of Ameri-can manners by the British press (though once or twice after an encounter with fellow-countrymen during the course of his consular duties he con-fided in his journal that perhaps there was something in what the English said about the uncouthness of certain Americans).

He was alternately attracted and repelled by England during the period of his consulship between 1853 and 1857. He admired the scenery and the ancient places, and the style in which the upper classes lived. But he detested the rain, the fog, the city dirt, the poverty, and the beggars. Cloud, composed of fog and coal-smoke, overhung Liverpool even in August, and he had never imagined such squalor as he found there among the poor, such depraved behaviour, such drunkenness, such hordes of beggars.

1 Nathaniel Hawthorne (1804–64), American novelist. Author of *The Scarlet Letter, The House with Seven Gables.*

"Here beggary is a system, and beggars are a numerous class, and make themselves, in a certain way, respected as such." He saw a man standing bareheaded and bare-legged, in the mud and misty weather, playing on a fife, in the hope that someone might pause to listen. He described the man without arms or legs who fixed the passer-by with a "gaze which is inconceivably hard to bear," the girl who crawled round the city on her hands and knees, the young man who touted a single dirty copy of *The Times* – all well-known figures in Liverpool in the 1850's. At first he was outraged by the English attitude that giving money to beggars did mischief, and that all of them could find a refuge somewhere if they chose, but later he was to be forced into this way of thinking himself.

Beggars apart, the amount of poverty distressed him. He spoke of bands of unemployed workers wandering round the suburbs asking for charity, and their meek, resigned demeanour. "They really seem to take their distress as their own misfortune and God's will, and impute it to nobody as a fault." Within the city there was poverty and squalor wherever one trod, with gin-shops every two or three steps.

He commented savagely on the ugliness of the middle class Englishman. Like Taine, he thought the English grossly over-ate. "I really pitied

THE OVERFED ENGLISH WOMAN WITH HER OVERFED DOG
Drawing by George du Maurier from *Punch*, 1892. Jokes about ugly, fat women were a favourite theme of the Victorian *Punch*.

the respectable elderly men who I saw walking about with such atrocities
hanging on their arms – the grim, red-faced monsters! Surely a man would
be justified in murdering them – in taking a sharp knife and cutting away
their mountainous flesh, until he has brought them into reasonable shape."
It was the penalty, he said, of a life of gross feeding, of much ale-guzzling
and beef-eating, and he was nostalgic for the trim, well-dressed figure of
the American woman.

In view of his generally unfavourable comments on the peculiarities of
the English way of life, his attitude towards the aristocracy is unexpected.
He realized that as a class they were doomed, but he saw it with regret. He
pointed out, truly enough, that it was the Crimean War (which was near-
ing its close as he wrote) that would at last put an end to aristocratic privilege.
Outraged by the incompetent way the war had been handled, the country
would never again allow its nobility to rule the nation in peace, or command armies in war, unless they were able as well as nobly born. "And
yet," he concluded sadly, "the nobles were never positively more noble
than now – never, perhaps, so chivalrous, so honourable, so highly cultivated." G. M. Young was also to speak some eighty years later in his
Victorian England: The Portrait of an Age of the life of the university-bred
classes in mid 19th century England as "the culminating achievement of
European culture."

Hippolyte Taine, the French critic and historian, visited England during
the 1860's and recorded his impressions in *Notes on England*. More than any
of the other visitors, he viewed it as an ineffably strange and foreign land –
as an Englishman might look wonderingly at the habits of Zulus. He
marvelled at the dirt, the rain, and the fog in England, at the size of the
English family (four children to him seemed a great many, and plenty of
families had far more than that), at the Puritan severity of a country where
there were large chained Bibles on railway stations for travellers to read
while waiting, where notices warned you to be decent, where intoxicating
liquor might not be served during times when the churches held their
services – this in a country whose national vice was drunkenness, and
where drink might be bought at all hours in the backrooms of taverns!

Like so many others, Taine was horrified by the drunkenness that he
saw continually about him; men lying dead drunk across the pavements,
women reeling down the streets, the prostitutes who begged for enough
money for a glass of gin. His appalled comments on the miseries of the poor

are quoted in a later chapter. It deeply wounded him that they were so down-trodden, so resigned to their state, so lacking in pride, that they slunk around ridiculously dressed in the rags of the discarded once-fashionable finery of the rich. "This tatterdemalion attire, which has clad four or five bodies in succession, I always find painful to see. It is degrading: by wearing it a person admits or declares himself to be one of the off-scourings of society."

Other things in England displeased him. He agreed with Hawthorne over the ugliness of so many Englishwomen; he shuddered at their large feet clad in sensible, mannish boots, and the way their teeth stuck out. "Some of them go to the extreme of ugliness and the grotesque, creatures with heron's feet, a stork's neck, and always that great frontage of white teeth, the prominent jaw of the carnivore." They seemed to have no idea how to dress: "the colours are outrageously crude, and the lines ungrace-ful." They might be pretty as young girls (though even then they lacked style and conversation) but "the noses of many young women easily turn red; and they bear too many children, which deforms them. You marry a blonde angel, slender and confiding; ten years later you may find your companion for a lifetime a housekeeper, a wet-nurse, a broody hen. I have in mind two or three such matrons, broad, stiff and without an idea in their heads; red faces, china-blue eyes, and enormous white teeth – like the tricolour flag."

Much of the English ugliness he put down to over-eating, particularly of meat. He supposed that the climate, the fog, the heavy manual and mental work that Englishmen undertook necessitated this; their organism was like an engine whose furnaces needed constant stoking with meat and spirits to keep the boiler going. He compared the men to shire horses, massive in bone and muscle, and spoke of the brutality of which they were capable. He witnessed this at its worst at that great beano of Victorian England – the race course at Epsom on Derby Day. Here he saw the English, patricians and plebians alike, all overflowing with animal spirits, betting heavily, drinking heavily, eating heavily; "nothing is barred to-day; it is an outlet for a whole year's constraint." After the races, the eating and drinking, after that the horseplay – the throwing of lobster shells and chicken bones, the boxing contests between the gentlemen, the gross behaviour contrasting so oddly with the serious faces and sober clothes. Taine also spoke of the thousands of prostitutes and street-walkers that the occasion

BOISTEROUS FUN AT THE EPSOM RACES

The artist, Doré, observes a respectable Englishman, top-hat and umbrella in hand, trying his strength at a race-ground side-show (*London,* 1872).

brought out. These indeed were a marked feature of Victorian London, but one very rarely referred to by the English writers.

Nevertheless Taine's impressions of England were by no means wholly unfavourable. He found in it much to commend warmly, much that he thought superior to France – and this for a Frenchman is not an admission easy to make. He admired the political system. It was stable and ran no risks, he considered, and he particularly remarked on the good sense whereby the government was put into the hands of the upper class, "which is the most capable of managing it well and which finds its natural employ-ment in such business instead of spoiling and growing decadent for want of an outlet, as with us." (Though this was a point of view which many Englishmen would have thought controversial.) He admired the orderly way in which the English conducted their affairs; reforms came about without revolution, the law was upheld by the people, the government could be freely and energetically criticized: "an establishment which is so firm in the saddle can stand assaults on it: speeches, meetings and leagues cannot overthrow it."

He spoke with admiration of the public spirit of the English and their willingness to take on work for the good of the community. He approved of the Church of England, its energy, the influence that it had over the community, and the fact that its clergy were free to marry. He was in favour, with reservations, of the English system of education at the public schools and universities, which gave the boys freedom and encouraged them to have a sense of responsibility, and he noticed with approval the influence that their religious beliefs had upon their behaviour. Though he could not admire Englishwomen's taste in clothes, nor their appearance, he conceded that they were very affable and kind and that you could feel far more at ease with them than with a Frenchwoman, and though they might not be so lively and witty you stood a better chance of sensible, serious conversation.

While he marvelled at the English devotion to sport, the seriousness with which they regarded it, and the extraordinary games that they played, he praised the attention that they gave to more intellectual matters, their eagerness to see foreign countries, the amount that was spent on books for the British Museum – seven or eight times the amount spent in France. He particularly dwelt on Oxford, praising its beauty, its antiquity, the feeling of the past that lingered there, and the esteem in which learning was held.

THE ENGLISH WEATHER
Running for shelter outside Westminster Abbey.
Illustration by Doré from *London*, 1872.

France made a poor showing beside this. "Poor Frenchmen, who are poor indeed, and live like men encamped! We belong to yesterday, ruined generation by generation . . . We demolished the past, and all had to be done over again. Here the new generation does not break with its predecessor: reforms are superimposed upon institutions; and the present, resting upon the past, continues it."

This pronouncement might be said to convey the essence of the Victorian achievement.

3 · The Aristocracy

"ARISTOCRACY" in its literal sense stems from two Greek words meaning the best, and the power, and signifies the government of a state by its best citizens. The dictionary defines it as the class to which such a ruling body belongs, and it is popularly used to mean all those who by birth or fortune rank above the rest of the community. In 1837 the aristocracy were the landowners. They were the ruling class of England, and it was necessary to be a landowner if one wanted to have political power. Disraeli[1] had to secure land before he could make much headway in political life, and was obliged to borrow money from the Duke of Portland in 1848 to buy the estate of Hughenden. Only then was he considered fit to lead the Tory party.

The landowners of the early Victorian period, although a blow had been struck at them with the Reform Act of 1832, still appeared to hold all the power and the privilege of the land. The greatest of them possessed splendid retinues and houses and had much influence in society. They were able, as has been described in an earlier chapter, to dominate elections. They also virtually ruled the area in which they lived – they were the lords lieutenant, the chief magistrates, the commanders of the militia, the Poor Law

---

1 Benjamin Disraeli (1804–81), first Earl of Beaconsfield, statesman and author. Tory Prime Minister first in 1868. The only English Prime Minister to publish novels while in office.

Old Buckingham Gate. Engraving by Gustave Doré.

Guardians. The comfort or discomfort, the content or discontent of thousands of people who lived on their land depended upon their goodwill.

There were too the smaller gentry, whose family might bear no title but who had passed their estate from father to son for centuries (Trollope wrote often of these). Not all of them had the power to sway elections and influence members of Parliament, but, as Flora Thompson[2] said of the lady of the manor of her childhood in the 1880's, "it would be almost impossible for any one born in this century to imagine [their] pride and importance." Known generically as "the gentry", the landowners of early Victorian England ruled England.

But although they held the monopoly of power their world was not closed to the outsider. A man could climb into it if he had the money and a forceful enough personality. He might not himself be accepted, but his children, given the right education and upbringing, would probably be able to mix with the gentry in adult life, and the origins of the family could well be completely forgotten by the time they grew up. De Tocqueville commented on this peculiarity of the English aristocracy, so very different from the French nobility whose ranks were closed to the outsider. With great riches, he said, anybody could become an aristocrat in England; and hitherto the English common man had not opposed the aristocracy because there were many who hoped that perhaps one day they might accumulate enough wealth to enter that charmed society themselves. The average member of the English middle class was immensely proud of any dealing he might have with the nobility and boasted about it. "The French wish not to have superiors. The English wish to have inferiors. The Frenchman constantly raises his eyes above him with anxiety. The Englishman lowers his beneath him with satisfaction."

Disraeli in *Sybil* illustrated how a man could hoist himself and his descendants into the ruling class by using wealth to good purpose. Earl de Mowbray is the son of a waiter who, in the 18th century, had gone out as valet with a gentleman to India, had bettered himself, done a little plundering, returned to England and bought a large estate and a close borough with it (that is, a borough where the landowner had the right of nominating the representative in Parliament). He had himself returned as member

2 Flora Thompson, author of *Lark Rise* (1939), *Over to Candleford* (1941) and *Candleford Green* (1943), a trilogy of her memories of a childhood spent in an Oxfordshire hamlet. See also p. 102.

1874 – A DUKE'S FUNERAL IN WESTMINSTER ABBEY

The dukes of Northumberland belonged to one of the oldest families in England and the death of one of them, however undistinguished personally, was a national event.

for this borough, made himself useful to the Prime Minister of the day at a time when every vote mattered, was rewarded with a baronetcy, bought a few more estates, and received a peerage. The son, Disraeli's Lord de Mowbray, is passionately anxious when he succeeds his father to rise higher in the peerage and ascend from a barony to an earldom.[1] Through his estates he can control the voting in six parliamentary boroughs; not only can he select the members to send to Parliament, but once his candidates are there he can supervise the way they vote. This makes him indispensable to the government. He is rewarded with the earldom he so ardently desires, and settles down to enjoy his honours, and is soon able to convince him/self that his pedigree is one of the most ancient in the land. Disraeli's ironical account of the origins of an aristocratic politician is not very far from the

1 This sort of ambition was fairly commonplace. The Grenville family, as ambitious as they were proud, bought up most of Buckinghamshire in the early years of the 19th century in order to gain themselves a dukedom, and achieved it only to crash into financial ruin in 1848.

truth. There was indeed a waiter who became a peer in much this manner.

Sybil was published in 1845, and Disraeli shows aristocracy after the old style. By the second half of the century corruption of the sort practised by Lord de Mowbray is no longer feasible. But Trollope in *Framley Parsonage* (1861) shows how a great landowner might use his political power and bring his influence to bear upon elections. The Duke of Omnium was, Trollope says, "as it were a great Lama, shut up in a holy of holies, inscrutible, invisible, inexorable – not to be seen by men's eyes or heard by their ears." There is a general election in sight; nobody suggests that he will influence the results of the contest in his own territory, "but, nevertheless, most men in the county believed that [the duke] could send his dog up to the House of Commons as member for West Barsetshire if it so pleased him." The small farmers and tradesmen might flatter themselves that they were voting Liberal because they *were* Liberal, but in fact they were voting that way because the Duke wished it, "and by an apprehension of evil if that Lama should arise and shake himself in his wrath. What might not come to the county if the Lama were to walk himself off, he with his satellites and armies and courtiers?"

Though they might not see the duke, the people of West Barsetshire see his agent, Mr. Fothergill, often enough. He tells the farmers how fortunate they are to have the Duke as a beneficent influence shedding prosperity on all around him, and keeping up the prices by the mere fact of his presence at Gatherum Castle. Men must be mad, he tells them, who would willingly fly in the Duke's face. He is indignant at the idea that he or the Duke are in any way influencing the voting.

"People would talk of things of which they understood nothing. Could anyone say that he had traced a single request for a vote home to the duke? All this did not alter the settled conviction in men's minds; but it had its effect, and tended to increase the mystery in which the duke's doings were enveloped. But to his own familiars, to the gentry immediately around him, Mr. Fothergill merely winked his eye. They knew what was what, and so did he."

But the political climate was changing. Foreign visitors had noticed that the aristocracy no longer wielded their old power. Prescott during his visit to England in 1850 observed the growing importance of manufacturers

1853 – "THE ORDINARY LEGAL EXPENSES OF AN ELECTION"

Punch mockingly draws attention to the corrupt practices of the time. In the elections of 1853 "several of the Members elected to the new Parliament had subsequently lost their seats for bribery".

and men of money. He also noticed how railways had broken down the isolation in which the landed gentry had lived. "Your railroad is the great leveller after all," he remarked. "Some of the old grandees make a most whimsical lament about it. Mrs. —'s father, who is a large proprietor, used to drive up to London with his family, to attend Parliament, with three coaches and four. But now-a-days he is tumbled in with the unwashed, in the first class, it is true, – no better than ours, however, – of the *railway* carriages; and then tumbled out again into a common cab with my Lady and all her little ones, like any of the common pottery."

Fashionable Londoners in their splendid equipages drive in Hyde Park. Engraving by Doré (*London,* 1872).

Disraeli, five years earlier, in *Sybil*, had shown with extravagant humour his aristocrats shaking their heads mournfully over the railways.

"A great revolution!" says Lord de Mowbray gloomily.
"Isn't it?" Lady Marney replies.
"I fear it has a very dangerous tendency to equality . . . Equality, Lady Marney, is not our métier. If we nobles do not make a stand against the levelling spirit of the age, I am at a loss to know who will fight the battle. You may depend upon it that these railroads are very dangerous things."

Lady Marney contributes an anecdote of her own. A friend of hers, she said, travelled up by rail to Birmingham with two most gentlemanly fellow-passengers. She had asked one of them if he could change seats with her, "and he was most politely willing to comply with her wishes, only it was necessary that his companion should move at the same time, for they were chained together! Two gentlemen, sent to town for picking a pocket at Shrewsbury races!"

All through Victoria's reign aristocratic power continued to diminish. The Duke of Omnium who succeeds the old duke – the great Lama whom we have already met – is a very different sort of man. We find him in later novels by Trollope. He is the central character of *The Prime Minister* (1876) and of *The Duke's Children* (1880), a sad, serious, grey personality, who labours with grinding energy at his life's work, the promotion of a decimal coinage, "without any motive more selfish than that of being counted in the roll of the public servants of England." He takes a very different attitude towards influencing the voting of his tenants. Part of this is due to his own conscientious nature, but times have changed too, since the easy corrupt days of the old duke, who ruled his lands after the 18th century fashion.

Plantagenet Palliser, the new duke, is determined that the electors in the local town of Silverbridge should vote for the candidate of their own choice. He even addresses a letter to them assuring them that "should they think fit to return a member pledged to oppose the Government of which I form a part, it would not in any way change my cordial feelings towards the town." When his own wife goes against his wishes and drops a half-hint to a local tradesman that such and such a Parliamentary candidate is the man of her choice, it is a matter of fearful grief and shame to the duke.

But the electors of Silverbridge are slower to change. They have so long been used to voting as the dukes pleased that they cannot shake off the habit. In *The Duke's Children* the young heir to the title, Lord Silverbridge, announces that he proposes to abandon the Whiggery of his ancestors and stand as a Tory candidate for the local constituency. It is an appalling blow to his father. But the men of Silverbridge are not perturbed. They do not particularly care whether they vote Whig or Tory, but they are anxious to please the Castle. So they are perfectly prepared to vote for young Lord Silverbridge whatever his political party, and if he decides to change from Tory back to the family tradition of Whig, why, this suits them well enough too.

What sort of people, then, were the aristocracy who ruled England until the middle classes took their power from them? Matthew Arnold styled them *The Barbarians*, comparing them to the barbarian hordes who brought about the downfall of the Roman Empire, and spoke of their sturdy individualism, their passion for personal liberty and for field sports, their cultivation of manly exercises, their vigour, good looks and fine complexion. He even compared their manners – "The chivalry of the Barbarians, with its characteristics of high spirit, choice manners, and distinguished bearing, – what is this but the attractive commencement of the politeness of our aristocratic class?" And Arnold said that when he went through the country and saw this or that beautiful country house crowning the landscape, " 'There,' I say to myself, 'is a great fortified post of the Barbarians.' "

Arnold might have compared them to the Barbarians in another particular, their habit of intermarriage, which so linked the aristocratic families that they have been compared to tribes. The men of these families would many of them have been educated at Eton or Harrow, and then at Oxford or Cambridge. Or perhaps they would have spent a few years in a smart regiment before retiring to their estates. For the younger sons who inherited no estates there might be a church living, a civil service post, or a seat in Parliament available – in the earlier decades of the century until such matters had been reformed. Their outlook and beliefs, their feeling about the way a gentleman should behave, would tend to follow the same pattern. The great 19th century aristocrats, one might say, belonged to the same club. And a feature of a large section of this club was Whiggery – a political opinion that one did not arrive at, as a general rule, by independent thought, but which one inherited from one's family. The Whigs held certain political opinions and pursued certain policies, but people did not become Whigs because they upheld these opinions; rather they upheld them because they were born into a Whiggish family. It was claimed with some truth that it was as difficult to become a Whig as to become a Jew. For the first thirty years of Victoria's reign the Whig aristocracy dominated the political scene.

The two great parties of England, the Whigs and the Tories, had arisen at the end of the 17th century, and were to turn by the end of the 19th into the Liberal and the Conservative parties. Broadly speaking, the Whigs were the great landed aristocrats, the descendants of the powerful nobility who had opposed James II and brought about the Revolution of 1688, while the Tories (though of course there were exceptions to this) were the lesser landowners, together with such elements as the clergy and the manufacturers. Their hatred and suspicion of each other's political policies often

THACKERAY'S COMMENT ON "LORDOLATRY"
"Lordolatry is part of our creed, and our children are brought up to respect the
'Peerage' as the Englishman's second Bible." *(The Book of Snobs.)*

went very deep. There is a story of a child of Whig parents who asked her
mother whether the Tories were born bad or just grew bad. "They are
born bad and grow worse," her mother told her with passionate feeling.

Trollope perfectly presents the emotion with which one party regarded
another when he describes in *Framley Parsonage* the fear and loathing that
Lady Lufton holds for the old Duke of Omnium. The Luftons of Framley
Court have owned land in Trollope's imaginary county of Barsetshire
for generations, they have always been "true blue" – that is, Tory. But
the Duke of Omnium, in the western half of Barsetshire, is a Whig.

"It was so thoroughly understood at Framley Court that the duke and all
belonging to him was noxious and damnable. He was a Whig, he was a
bachelor, he was a gambler, he was immoral in every way, he was a man of
no Church principle, a corrupter of youth, a sworn foe of young wives, a
swallower up of small men's patrimonies; a man whom mothers feared for

their sons, and sisters for their brothers; and worse again, whom fathers had cause to fear for their daughters, and brothers for their sisters; – a man who, with his belongings, dwelt, and must dwell, poles asunder from Lady Lufton and her belongings!"

Lady Lufton believes him to be the impersonation of Lucifer on earth; in her mind – as the paragraph above shows – his politics and his morals are inseparable.

Trollope in his novels about the Dukes of Omnium beautifully illustrates the outlook of the great Whig noblemen. We have already seen Whiggery after the 18th century pattern in the old Duke. And Whiggery with its rigid class barriers is still part of the make-up of his successor Plantagenet Palliser. Though he regards himself as the antithesis of his uncle, Whiggery is in his bones and blood, not a political creed but a social caste. It is a matter of great grief to him when his heir, Lord Silverbridge, decides to become a Tory, and when his daughter announces that she wishes to marry a Tory.

" 'I suppose it is as – as – as respectable to be a Conservative as a Liberal,' says Lady Mary faintly.

'I don't know that at all,' said the Duke angrily."

But it is an even greater catastrophe when Lord Silverbridge proposes to marry an American. Silverbridge's proposed bride is beautiful, well-educated, and charming in her manner. She is wealthy and she has not even an American accent, but the Duke feels he belongs to "an aristocracy which, if all exclusiveness were banished from it, must cease to exist." He does not reflect that the English aristocracy had probably only survived from the very fact that it was not rigidly exclusive, nor does he choose to remember that the political beliefs of the Whig party, at any rate on paper, are liberal and progressive, and that Whigs were even suspected by their Tory opponents of an earlier generation of supporting the French revolution. In his public life he would not dream of making any difference between himself and somebody whose grandmother was a washerwoman. But the thought of this charming and spirited young American (whom he admits to liking) becoming a future Duchess of Omnium fills him with appalled despair.

Disraeli saw the great Whig families as a selfish clique who spent far too much time pleasuring in the smart London social world, allying themselves politically with the Irish, with shopkeepers, with manufacturers – people with whom they could have no sympathy whatever – merely for the sake of holding on to power. He believed in the Tory aristocrats and squires who stayed on their country estates devoting themselves to the interests of their tenants and ruling the lower classes like a benevolent and despotic father. In *Sybil, or the Two Nations*, one of the greatest of the Victorian political novels, published in 1845, a time when the miseries of the poor were at their height, and the difference between the privileged class and the workers at their most marked, Disraeli gives a satirical account of a great Whig family who gained an earldom by an adroit political move in the 17th century "and from that time until the period of our history, though the Marney family had never produced one individual eminent for civil or military abilities, though the country was not indebted to them for a single statesman, orator, successful warrior, great lawyer, learned divine, eminent author, illustrious man of science, they had contrived, if not to engross any great share of public admiration and love, at least to monopolize no contemptible portion of public money and public dignities."

The hero of Disraeli's *Sybil*, Charles Egremont, grows up on the eve of the great change, i.e., the Reform Bill, "that, whatever was its purpose or have been its immediate results, at least gave the first shock to the pseudo-aristocracy of this country. Then all was blooming sunshine and odour; not a breeze disturbing the meridian splendour. Then the world was not only made for a few, but a very few. One could almost tell upon one's fingers the happy families who could do anything, and might have everything. A schoolboy's ideas of the Church then were fat livings, and of the State, rotten boroughs. To do nothing and get something formed a boy's ideal of a manly career."

As Victoria's reign moved on the privileges were taken from the hands of the few and distributed more evenly. True, the aristocracy continued to govern. The new voters from the manufacturing towns recognised that the aristocracy had the leisure and the money for Parliament, and so even in the 1860's and 1870's we still find the Cabinets largely made up of members of those noble families who had traditionally held office. The difference now was that they held office because a powerful new class

THE DECLINE OF THE ARISTOCRATIC LANDOWNER

Punch (whose figure is seen on the left) in a cartoon of 1850 attacks the selfishness of the landowner. A coroneted peer is shown bemoaning Free Trade and the poverty it has brought him.

wished them to do so, and they could be thrust aside when that class felt that their day was over.

Their privileges were dwindling. They might still have their London mansions, their country acres, their grouse moors and castles in Scotland, their hunting boxes in the Midlands, their yachts, and their liveried servants, but by the late decades of Victoria's reign they were no longer the power in the land.

It was perhaps the Crimean War that toppled them from their secure positions in the Army and the civil service. The Army since the 17th century had been unashamedly aristocratic. Commissions had to be bought in the first place, and promotion thereafter depended not upon ability nor seniority, but upon the ability to pay. Officers of experience and proven competence were left in junior positions while men of wealth bought their way upwards. The War Office even allowed their regiments to be sold. Lord Cardigan, who led the Light Brigade in their disastrous charge against the Russian guns at the battle of Balaclava in 1854, paid £25,000 to the retiring colonel for the command of his first regiment. His brother-in-law, Lord Lucan, bought the command of his at a cost, it was stated in *The Times*, of between £35,000 and £40,000.

Ridiculous as it might seem to the outsider, there was a purpose in this. England had seen enough of Cromwell's Model Army to be terrified of military dictatorship, and was determined that never again should professional soldiers be allowed to dominate the nation. It was held that the

THE MILITARY DANDY

General. Mr. de Bridoon, what is the general use of cavalry in modern warfare?"
Mr. de Bridoon. "Well, I suppose to give tone to what would otherwise be a mere vulgar brawl!"

Drawing from *Punch,* 1892.

men to encourage as officers and commanders were the wealthy landed gentry who would look upon the Army as a part-time occupation, rather than landless military adventurers with no other interests to distract them. And the fact was that the British Army, whose fighting rank and file were second to none, had won every major European war they had engaged in since the Restoration. During the first half of the 19th century any attempt to attack the purchase system was held to be a direct encouragement to revolution, and when Britain entered upon the Crimean War in 1854 it was with dandified young officers who were used to lounging round their London clubs and to riding after fox hounds, and who paid devoted attention to the arrangement of their epaulettes and the fit of their trousers, but who had never seen active service. No more had their commanders, who flung themselves into the campaign as though it were a parade in Hyde Park.

The miseries, humiliations, and sufferings endured during the Crimean War as a direct result of blundering incompetence both among the commanders in the field and in the government departments at home cured England of the desire to remain amateur. Dickens acknowledged that his thrusts at the imaginary Circumlocution Office in *Little Dorrit* were

THE BARNACLES AND THEIR ALLIES
Members of the English ruling class discuss whom they propose should fill three vacant seats in Parliament. Illustration from *Little Dorrit*.

made with the bitterness of the Crimean War in his mind. He wrote of the stranglehold that the aristocratic families had upon government departments up to the middle of the century.

"The Barnacle family had for some time helped to administer the Circumlocution Office. The Tite Barnacle Branch, indeed, considered themselves in a general way as having vested rights in that direction, and took it ill if any other family had much to say to it. The Barnacles were a very high family, and a very large family. They were dispersed all over the public offices, and held all sorts of public places. Either the nation was under a load of obligation to the Barnacles, or the Barnacles were under a load of obligation to the nation. It was not quite unanimously settled which; the Barnacles having their opinion, the nation theirs."

Political reforms took power from the landowners, agricultural depressions towards the end of the century reduced their income. The nobleman cut down his establishment, modified his way of life. By the opening decades of this century all influence except that which mere wealth could give him, and the deference that is paid to an ancient name, had vanished. The aristocrat was on his way to becoming that rather sad figure that we meet in the mid 20th century, reduced to conducting tourists round his house in order to keep death watch beetle out of its timbers.

Trollope in his political novels shows us the old Duke of Omnium and his successor, the conscientious highminded Plantagenet Palliser, the great tragedy of whose life is the discovery that the Whigs have chosen him to lead their party because of his illustrious name, not because of his own abilities or achievements. What of the future generations of Pallisers, what sort of dukes are they likely to make? We meet Plantagenet's heir in *The Duke's Children*, that young Lord Silverbridge who, as has been already said, appals his father by wishing to become a Tory and to marry an American. He is an amiable, conscientious lad and one can infer that he will settle down to being a duke of the late Victorian kind, with little political influence but a great deal of money (derived partly from his wife's inheritance), who will devote himself to running his estates, entertaining, and sport. As a young man he is wild, of course – but it was considered unnatural and unwholesome if a young nobleman was not. He is sent down from Oxford for having, in an outburst of aristocratic high spirits, painted the Dean of Christ Church's house red. He is also apt to lose large sums of money – large even for a duke's heir – at horse races, though his father considers it a great relief that he has persuaded the boy to keep out of the hands of the money-lenders, the horror of all wealthy fathers of improvident sons.

Silverbridge, in fact, follows the pattern of many of the real life young aristocracy of the period. So does his young brother, Lord Gerald, at the bottom well-meaning, but on the surface irritatingly wild and reckless. In an age when the universities were still heavily populated with the wealthy and idle, he has contrived so to offend his tutor at Cambridge that he has been sent down. Lord Gerald has defied the tutor by coming up from Cambridge, when expressly forbidden to do so, to see his brother's horse race in the Derby. This still might have been covered up had he returned to Cambridge that night, but he stays on at the Derby dinner saying that he knows the train will not start at the time named. "There were a lot of fellows who were dining about everywhere and they would never get to the station by the hour fixed." But trains no longer wait for the aristocracy. " 'Who on earth would have thought that they'd have been so punctual?'," says the irritated young nobleman, and his brother asks him why he did not make them run a special train to get him down to Cambridge. " 'They wouldn't give me one.' After that it was apparent to all of them that what had just happened had done more to ruffle our hero's temper than his failure and loss at the races."

The aristocrat's privileges are falling away from him; special trains no longer run at his will, dukes are powerless against the decision of a college tutor to send their sons down. The old order has changed.

4 · *Society Life*

THERE were many Victorian novelists of the lesser sort who dwelt lovingly on life in high society as they imagined it: a whirl of balls and grand receptions during the London season; a retreat to the velvety lawns and the spreading cedars of one's ancestral home in July, when one took care to fill the house with congenial friends; August perhaps in a Scottish castle while the sportsmen shot grouse; a visit to a foreign watering-place – Baden Baden, Pau, or Mentone; back to England for the opening of the fox-hunting season; more house parties over Christmas, which with the hunting and the shooting could tide one over until the London season began again in the spring.

Even among the wealthiest of the upper classes, however, there were only a small proportion who flitted between Mayfair, their grouse moor, their hunting box, and the Continent; who, in short, lived the life of high society as the novelists understood it. There were others who might spend ten months of the year stolidly on their country estate, with two months perhaps in London for "the season", and there were those who played

A box at the Opera. Engraving by Doré

no part in London society life at all, the small country gentry whose circle of acquaintances was drawn entirely from the other gentry of the neighbourhood within driving distance.

Trollope was never a member of fashionable society, but he understood it better perhaps than any writer of his time. He could describe convincingly the high society of London, the balls, receptions, the political gossip, the conversation in the smart clubs. He could convey the atmosphere of a house party at one of the great country houses, or show the life led by those landowners whose interests were bounded by the limits of their estates, or those who lacked the money to come up to London and who led a stupefying existence in the country, surrounded by their discontented wife and daughters. And what impresses us and seems to have the ring of truth is

Punch OBSERVES ARISTOCRATIC BOREDOM
Future Duke. "What are you goin' to do this mornin' eh?"
Future Earl. "Oh, I dunno. Rot about, I s'pose, as usual."
Future Duke. "Oh, but I say, that's so rotten."
Future Earl. "Well, what else is there to do, you rotter?"

the dullness of it all, the difficulty of filling one's time, the flat, trite conversation with its limited range of topics.

Lord Ernest Hamilton, who left reminiscences of midVictorian London society, made the same point. Everything was dull. The newspapers – The *Times*, *Morning Post*, or *The Standard* – dealt only with Court news, social functions, and political speeches. Conversation consisted mainly of anecdotes of a very decorous sort. References to seasickness (or *maldemer* as it was genteelly called) were daring and produced shouts of laughter. When the anecdotes were exhausted, then food was discussed, or health. "Platitudes, no matter how threadbare, were always sure of a warm welcome. How wonderful the Prime Minister's speech was! How cold the East wind was! What a wonderful cook the Duchess of Sutherland had! How sad it was that poor Lady Bloomsbury's cold was no better." Conversation with the young unmarried girl, newly "come out" – that is, released from the schoolroom at the age of eighteen or so, and now admitted into adult society – was particularly trying, if one could drag a word out of her at all. "She is one of those delicious creatures who, in spite of not being married, are actually conversable," says a young man in Disraeli's *Vivian Grey*. And Taine describes a young English girl in a Paris drawingroom, in an "illfitting cassocklike white dress, so that her figure looked like a faggot tied up in a sack. The whole evening she was as mute as Cinderella among the splendours and surpassing elegance of the beauties and dresses all about her." Taine, like other visiting foreigners, found the upper class Englishwoman inelegant and dull. "She is not attractive and one is quickly bored in her company. Imagine a very beautiful, rosy peach, moderately wellflavoured, beside an aromatic strawberry full of high flavour," he remarked, comparing the English with the Frenchwoman.

Surtees[1] in *Mr. Sponge's Sporting Tour* writes of how wearyingly time can drag in an early Victorian country household. "What a dreary time is that which intervenes between the arrival of a guest and the dinner hour, in the dead winter months in the country. The English are a desperate people for overweighting their conversational powers. They have no idea of penning up their small talk, and bringing it to bear in generous flow upon one particular hour; but they keep dribbling it out throughout the livelong day, wearying their listeners without benefiting themselves." Then

1 Robert Smith Surtees (1803–64). Author of humorous sporting novels.

follows an account of a winter evening at Jawleyford Grange, in vast, cold rooms where such heat as the fires give out is sucked up the chimneys; with strangled, fitful conversation about the prospects for hunting next day, and a heavy dinner cooked after the English style and served on the family plate in an icy dining room. Mr. Jawleyford and his wife and daughters come off better than the guest for they rarely have such a novelty as a visitor to interrupt the tedium of their lives.

Tedious though it might be, country life filled a large proportion of the year for the Victorian upper classes. There were few of them who lived permanently in their London houses. To be smart it was certainly necessary to be in London during May and June, but it was equally necessary to be out of London by August, and to the 19th century gentry the country was their proper home, and sport their principal occupation when they were there. Visiting foreigners commented on the extravagant English devotion to sport and country life. William Prescott was one of the more kindly. "The English love their old castles and country seats with a patriotic love," he wrote in 1850. "They are fond of country sports. Every man shoots or hunts. No man is too old to be in the saddle some part of the day, and men of seventy years and more follow the hounds and take a five-barred gate at a leap. The women are good whips, are fond of horses and dogs, and other animals. Duchesses have their cows, their poultry, their pigs, – all watched over and provided with accommodations of Dutch-like neatness." Even landowners in whom the sporting instinct was not strong had to pretend to show a decent interest in the local hunt if they were not to be outlawed by their more sporting neighbours. And the man who preferred pheasants to hunting and allowed his gamekeeper to banish foxes from his woods and stop up the foxes' earths was regarded as a public enemy and would have to endure the execrations of the fox-hunters around him.

Sport then was not only the pleasure of the Victorian landowner, it was also something of a duty and was taken very seriously. Trollope caricatures the deadly earnest English sporting gentleman in *The Duke's Children*. Reginald Dobbes is such a man. "Sport was the business of his life, and he thoroughly despised all who were not sportsmen. He fished and shot and hunted during nine or ten months of the year, filling up his time as best he might with coaching, polo, and pigeon-shooting. He regarded it as a great duty to keep his body in the finest possible condition....

HUNTING ENTHUSIASTS
Three farmhands.

But it never occurred to him that his whole life was one of self-indulgence. He could walk his thirty miles with his gun on his shoulder as well now as he could ten years ago; and being sure of this, was thoroughly contented with himself."

Victorian novels abound in references to sport. Indeed, fox-hunting produced a literature of its own. Trollope provided plenty of hunting

HUNTING ENTHUSIASTS
A gouty local tradesman and his wife. *Illustrated London News*, 1846.

scenes in his novels and Surtees and Whyte-Melville[1] treat of little else. Enthusiasm for fox-hunting infected all levels of society in the country. Flora Thompson in *Lark Rise* describes how the labourers in the fields would join in the excitement as hounds poured over the fields where they were working, and would cheer and shout encouragement. Cobbett[2] described the excitement before a meet of hounds in a Hampshire village in 1825, an "anxiously looked-for event. I have seen no man, or boy, who did not talk about it. There had been a false report about it; the hounds did *not come*; and the anger of the disappointed people was very great. At last, however, the *authentic* intelligence came, and I left them all as happy as if all were young and all just going to be married."

Trollope refers to the freedom of fox-hunting from the class distinctions that otherwise proliferated in Victorian social life. "The non-hunting world," he wrote, "is apt to think that hunting is confined to country gentlemen, farmers, and rich strangers; but any one . . . will find that there are in the crowd attorneys, country bankers, doctors, apothecaries . . . maltsters, millers, butchers, bakers, innkeepers, auctioneers, graziers, builders, . . . stockbrokers, newspaper editors, artists, and sailors. . . . Beneath [the master] there is freedom and equality for all, with special honour only for the man who is known to be specially good at some portion of the day's work." And in real life there was a pauper in receipt of out-door relief who was a regular follower of the Pytchley hounds on a bony old screw of a horse, and an Oxford chimney sweep who boasted how he rode to hounds with a duke.

Very rarely in the Victorian novel do we come across any opposition to the Englishman's traditional country pursuits. Hardy's *Tess of the D'Urbervilles* provides an exception. Tess, wandering through the country seeking a place as a dairymaid, comes to the edge of a plantation where pheasants lie wounded and dying. She realizes that a shooting party has been here, and these are the wounded birds who have escaped them.

"She had occasionally caught glimpses of these men in girlhood, looking over hedges, or peering through bushes, strangely accoutred, a blood-thirsty light in their eyes. She had been told that, rough and brutal as they

1 George John Whyte-Melville (1821–78). Author of novels dealing with military, sporting and society life.
2 William Cobbett (1762–1835), essayist, politician and agriculturist.

seemed just then, they were not like this all the year round, but were, in fact quite civil persons save during certain weeks of autumn and winter, when, like the inhabitants of the Malay Peninsula, they ran amuck, and made it their purpose to destroy life – in this case harmless feathered creatures, brought into being by artificial means solely to gratify these propensities."

Country life was in many ways a demanding life for the landowner. It would be difficult for him to escape the notice of his tenants and his neigh-bours, or to lead a secluded and anonymous life. He would be expected to ride out and meet his farmers, to entertain the other gentry, to take a decent interest in sport, and play his part in the administration of the district. The tenants would expect to rejoice with their landlord on all happy occasions, and to help him celebrate weddings, birthdays and such anniversaries, when there would be much pealing of bells, oxen roasted whole perhaps, and heavy dinners would be provided by the squire and heavy speeches made. The twelve-year-old Lord Amberley (Bertrand Russell's father) left an account of how his parents' wedding anniversary was celebrated in 1855.

"May 20 B.D. [i.e. before dinner] – This was Mama's wedding day, and the schoolchildren are to have a lottery this afternoon. We flew the kite and got 20 other kites ready for the children. A.D. [after dinner]. At 4.30 they marched up. First they went to Mama, then to the bowling-green where they played at bowls till they had to go to tea. They all sat down in a round on the grass at the bottom of the lawn. After tea they played a game, then went to the bowling-green where we had the lottery. Then they all stood in a line, and sang 'God Save the Queen'. This was the end so they all marched off. But before they sang they had given three cheers for Mama and three for the young ladies of the family (which I forgot to say)."

Entertaining was a great feature of country life. There were plenty of landowners who could afford to entertain on a lavish scale, and fill their houses with forty or more guests who might stay for two weeks at a time. Sport would be provided. At Eaton Hall in the 1860's the Duke of Westminster would ask his guests in the evening whether they preferred to shoot or to hunt the following day. Those who wished to hunt would be provided with an excellent hunter, and the shooting party would be

BANQUET AT ALNWICK CASTLE, 1867

1600 guests were entertained at a dinner to mark the coming of age of the Duke of
Northumberland's heir. A temporary building (shown in this engraving from
The Illustrated London News) was added to the guest-hall for the occasion.

driven out in a brake to the covert-side where pheasants put up by the
beaters would already be streaming across the sky, to be shot down in their
hundreds. As such parties the ladies were provided with drives during
the daytime, or croquet and archery at the appropriate season, and in the
evening there would be music and cards and billiards. They might well –
and many of them confessed it – be suffocated with boredom. When the
ladies had taken themselves to bed the men would change into special
clothes and retreat into a room set aside for smoking; the smell of cigar
and cigarette smoke was not to be inhaled by the delicate nostrils of
females.

When William Prescott came over to England in 1850 he was entertained by the Duke of Northumberland at Alnwick Castle, and his
letters home give a very fair idea of the scale on which such a landowner
lived. Of dinner on the first evening he wrote: "There was a multitude of

servants, and the liveries, blue, white and gold, of the Duke were very rich. We had also our own servants to wait on us. The table was loaded with silver. Every plate was silver, and everything was blazoned with the Northumberland arms."

He was impressed by the turnout of the household – a hundred or more – at prayers in the chapel the following morning, conducted by the Duke's chaplain, and commented that prayers were read in all the English houses where he had stayed, the master of the house officiating if there were no chaplain. He attended a public dinner of all the great tenant farmers in the county, where the Duke and his guests presided over an assembly of a thousand people in a building specially erected for the occasion.

"Another day we went in to see the peasantry of the great tenants dine, some sixteen hundred in number, or rather we saw them for half an hour after dinner. The Duke and Duchess took the head of the hall, and I thought the people, dressed in their best, to whom the dinner was given, as they drank off healths to their noble hearts, would have gone mad with enthusiasm. I nearly did so from the noise. The Duke, on allusion to his wife, brought her forward; and she bowed to the multitude. It was altogether a pretty sight."

This was the Duke known as "Algernon the Benevolent" whose death in 1865 was reported by the *Newcastle Journal* as shedding "a gloom and sorrow in the north whose dark shadow will fall upon a generation to come." Seven thousand people filed past his coffin at the lying in state, and the bells of York Minster were tolled as the funeral train passed through the station.

To be popular and successful as a landowner, then, a man needed to be fond of entertaining and sport, and possessed of an easy, cheerful manner with his equals and inferiors. If he were blessed with these qualities his tenants and peasantry would be willing to overlook the fact that he was readier with promises than with action when it came to the repair and upkeep of their farms and cottages.

Belchamber, a novel of late Victorian society by Howard Sturgis,[1] published in 1904, describes the predicament of a young man who is not

1 Howard Overing Sturgis (1855–1920). Edwardian host and author of three novels, of which *Belchamber* is the only one now remembered.

endowed with the qualities so desirable in the holder of an ancient title and owner of vast estates. By nature the young Lord Belchamber is a scholarly recluse, who would have wished to spend his days as a Cambridge academic. But his family dismiss this idea as utterly impossible, and are reluctant to let him stay even long enough to take his degree. Dutifully he returns to Belchamber, and finds to his surprise that the affairs of the estate interest him deeply, and he busies himself with schemes for the welfare of his tenants. But they do not like him, they are suspicious of his intellectual approach, take his shyness for pride, and despise him for his indifference to sport. Everybody laments that his younger brother, Arthur, is not the marquis. "A finer-looking young fellow it would have been hard to find at this time, tall and fair and ruddy, of athletic proportions, and agreeable manners, a most attractive personality." Arthur is a superb horseman and a good shot, he has an easy manner with the tenants, and even his vices seem attractive in a nobleman – his reckless extravagance and his pursuit of women. But Arthur is the younger son and as such has to stand back and watch, with considerable bitterness, his brother enjoying the privileges of wealth and high rank. He and the tenants are convinced that he would make the better marquis. Lord Belchamber would willingly yield the title and the estates to him, but English law and custom is inexor- able, and Arthur has to retreat into the background and do the best he can on the allowance that his brother makes him.

Taine remarked on the great difference that the English aristocracy made between their heirs and their other sons and cited the example of two brothers up at Oxford together, the elder with £100 a year more than his younger brother, merely because he was the heir. And Victorian fiction is full of younger sons struggling with an allowance they consider wholly inadequate, while the eldest brother enjoys the whole of the family estate. They are especially prominent characters in Trollope's novels, dejectedly lounging round their London clubs, running up debts they know they cannot pay, and listlessly discussing the heiresses they might marry if only the girl's father will agree.

Trollope also shows younger sons who are worthy but penniless and with no prospect of an income large enough to support a wife, mournfully abandoning the idea of marriage to the girl they love, since however dearly two people love each other it would be unthinkable to marry on £600 a year, and equally outside the social tradition for a man of this sort to earn

THE UNWANTED YOUNGER SON

First Juvenile. "May I have the pleasure of dancing with you, Miss Alice?"
Second Juvenile. "Ah, no – thanks! I never dance with younger sons!"

(*Punch,* 1863.)

his living in commerce or trade. Very little would be open to him. He might be lucky enough to secure by aristocratic influence some Civil Service post of the sort that Dickens' Barnacle family found for themselves, but Victorian families were large and the number of such positions was not infinite. He might go into the Church if a family living was available – there were many Victorian squires whose younger brothers dwelt nearby in the parsonage. Mrs. Gladstone's family owned Hawarden, and her brother Henry was Rector of Hawarden parish, with an income of £4000 a year and a rectory as large as a sizeable country house. There was the Army, but that required money; no officer could live on his pay alone. A few younger sons of great houses might go in for politics – Lord John Russell, Lord Randolph Churchill, Lord George Bentinck, all of them dukes' sons, are distinguished examples; but for this sort of career quite considerable wealth was needed.

Disraeli's protegé, Lord Henry Lennox, is an example of the dilemma of the younger son. He was a son of the Duke of Richmond, and Member of Parliament for Chichester – though that of course demanded an income rather than brought one in. He had run through his own money and felt that only two courses were now open to him; he must either secure a profitable post in the government, or secure an heiress, and with this in mind he was forever pestering Disraeli for help. Disraeli could never find him the first, and the young man seems to have been thoroughly inept as a wooer. He asked Disraeli to back him in his struggle to carry off a Rothschild daughter, having already failed with a Spanish princess who was forbidden to marry a Protestant, and failed again with the daughter of a *nouveau riche* Scot whom his father the Duke persisted in snubbing. But Disraeli could not help with the wealthy Rothschild either, and Lord Henry remained unmarried to the end.

These younger sons were further unfortunate in that they would have inherited expensive tastes and pleasures, which probably did not appear extravagant to them, since they had been brought up in this style – as would all their friends – at home, at school and at the university. Sport, for instance, could absorb an amazing amount of money, and sport, as has been said, played a large part in the life of the English upper classes. "November to April, Melton, then a month's salmon fishing in Ireland and Punchestown; in May, June, and July, London; then Goodwood and Cowes; then 'grouse' somewhere, and Doncaster; next a broken week or two at Newmarket and a little schooling of young Irish horses after cubs. Such as this was the determination to pleasure of tens of thousands – of really the pick of our young fellows." This was a Victorian's description of how those of his contemporaries with sporting tastes spent their year in a round of fox-hunting, fishing, the London season, racing, shooting, and then hunting again.

It was clearly the sort of life that required a considerable income, and a large income was what few younger sons possessed. But the Victorian upper classes were rarely discouraged from enjoying themselves by lack of money. Disraeli was never out of debt to the end of his life, but this did not prevent his living in sumptuous style. Mr. Sowerby in *Framley Parsonage* "was one of those men who are known to be very poor – as poor as debt can make a man – but who, nevertheless, enjoy all the luxuries which money can give. It was believed that he could not live

A FASHIONABLE STREET IN THE LONDON "SEASON"
From *The Illustrated London News,* 1847.

in England out of jail but for his protection as a member of Parliament; and yet it seemed that there was no end to his horses and carriages, his servants and retinue. He had been at this work for a great many years, and practice, they say, makes perfect." And when his creditors finally catch up with Mr. Sowerby and send the bailiffs to his house with peremptory demands for £500, he still has enough money in his pocket to take a cab across the road to see his sister. "It is a remarkable thing," comments Trollope, "with reference to men who are distressed for money – distressed as was now the case with Mr. Sowerby – that they never seem at a loss for small sums, or deny themselves those luxuries which small sums purchase. Cabs, dinners, wine, theatres, and new gloves are always at the command of men who are drowned in pecuniary embarrassments, whereas those who don't owe a shilling are so frequently obliged to go without them! It would seem that there is no gratification so costly as that of keeping out of debt."

George Hotspur in another of Trollope's novels, *Sir Harry Hotspur*, is similarly untroubled by his lack of money. "He was living in a bachelor's set of rooms, at this time, in St. James's Street. . . . During the last winter he had horses in Northamptonshire. . . . At the present time he had a horse for Park riding, and he looked upon a good dinner, with good wine, as being due to him every day, as thoroughly as though he earned it. That he had never attempted to earn a shilling since the day on which he had ceased to be a soldier, now four years since, the reader will hardly require to be informed."

Mr. Sowerby relied on the moneylenders to get him over any little difficulty of lack of income; George Hotspur on running up debts with his tradesmen. "As for getting goods from tradesmen without any hope or thought of paying for them, that with him was so much a thing of custom, – as indeed it was also with them, – that he was almost to be excused for considering it the normal condition of life for a man in his position."

Thackeray in *Vanity Fair* devotes two chapters to "How to Live Well on Nothing a Year", showing how Colonel Rawdon Crawley and his wife with no income at all, live splendidly and spend lavishly. "How the Crawleys got the money which was spent upon the entertainments with which they treated the polite world, was a mystery which gave rise to some conversation at the time," remarked Thackeray, and explained it thus: "The truth is, that by economy and good management – by a sparing use of ready money and by paying scarcely anybody, – people can manage, for a time at least, to make a great show with very little means." The wretched man who has let his house to the Crawleys is utterly ruined, his children flung on the streets, and himself driven into a debtors' prison.

It was the money lenders that wealthy Victorian fathers dreaded for their sons. Let a young man run his head into that noose, and he well might never struggle free. He would sign a bill promising to return the loan at such and such a date, and when the date fell due, he would, being still penniless, borrow a little more money and make renewed promises of repayment at a higher rate of interest, and finally with thousands owing and a savage interest exacted, might be forced to reveal his appalling predicament to his father. This is a situation that occurs frequently in Trollope's novels. The really unscrupulous young man might try to borrow money by "post-obits" – that is, on the security of the money he hoped to receive upon the death of some relation. Disraeli in the course of his wild youth became involved with money-lenders and never fought clear of them until long after he had become famous and successful. Then a wealthy young Tory, asking what he could do to help the Tory party, was told that he could buy up Dizzy's debts from the money-lenders and lend him the money himself at a reasonable rate of interest.

London society life changed considerably during the course of the Victorian period. It had long been the tradition for the wealthy land-owner to spend certain months of the year in London, and many owned houses in the Mayfair district of London which they would occupy during the season. The season was an important part of the social year and coincided roughly with the sitting of Parliament, for the people

A LONDON BALL
From *The Illustrated London News,* 1847.

who were prominent in society were also those who ruled the country. Everybody of any social pretension felt obliged to be in London in May, June, and July, and equally obliged to be out of it by August.

In the 40's, 50's, and 60's the fashionable circle was comparatively small. There were a few great houses – Devonshire House, Lansdowne House, Harcourt House, Stafford House, Chesterfield House, Montagu House – and most of the people that one met there would be connected with political life; these were the days when the landed aristocracy were the rulers. Entertaining might be done with political ends in view. Lady Palmerston was responsible for much of her husband's popularity as Prime Minister in the later years of his life. She received guests not only at evening functions, but during the day, and wrote all her invitations in her own hand. It was the climax of social distinction to receive one of these. When Lord John Russell dismissed Palmerston from the Foreign Office in 1851, Lady Palmerston retaliated by giving a party at which was present every person of any political, social or intellectual distinction in London, and *The Times* played up to her by printing a complete list of her guests under the title "The Expelled Minister".

Trollope's Duchess of Omnium, the beautiful Glencora, is similarly determined to support her husband. When he is made Prime Minister she tells herself that she will devote all her life to making him popular, to entertaining his political friends and allies so lavishly that no one thus entertained can do anything but support him. To this end she spends hundreds of thousands of pounds on parties in London, on gatherings at Gatherum Castle, the vast and forbidding official residence of the Dukes of Omnium which all the family detest and only use once a year for large house parties. The only figure of any importance who is absent from these receptions is the Duke himself, who perhaps after a solitary dinner of a beefsteak and a potato in his own rooms, may steel himself to creep like a grey shadow into the hubbub of the throng that his wife is entertaining, supposedly for his sake; nod to a few old friends and then creep away again.

The great noblemen of the middle years of the 19th century could live in great state in London. Lord Ernest Hamilton in *The Halycon Era* wrote of the sort of establishment that might be kept up in the 1860's. His father was the Marquis (later the Duke) of Abercorn, and the family when in London lived in Chesterfield House, a mansion with a garden big enough for a little boy to gallop his pony round the gravel walks, and with stables and coach-houses covering a large area.

"The most familiar object was my mother's barouche, a noble equipage indeed, dark crimson panelled and hung high up on C springs. The spokes of the wheels were striped in crimson, black and yellow, and the heavy silver harness was relieved by huge rosettes of dark blue and white. (How we despised people whose harness was of common brass!) High up on the box sat the great Busk [the head coachman] in breeches and silk stockings . . . and after a while an equally splendid footman climbed up to keep him company and off the black-brown horses would prance." . . .

"The coach-house hid a host of carriages of one kind or another, but the two that eclipsed all the others in splendour were, of course, the State Coach and the Chariot – pronounced Charyot. On the rare occasions when the Coach lurched out of the stables, the black-brown horses were almost obliterated by the splendour of their trappings. More pre-cariously perched than ever on the high, swaying box, now superbly draped in pink samite, or something of the sort, Busk, radiant in pink and silver and with a three-cornered hat crowning his white wig, stared imperturbably into the distance. Joseph and Thomas, dressed up to match, and only moderately drunk, took up their undignified position on the spring board at the back, the gates were thrown wide and out tumbled the great equipage."

The state coach would only be used on great occasions, such as a reception at Buckingham Palace. The chariot resembled it, except that it had two seats only and a glass front. The barouche was used by the ladies for taking the air in Hyde Park, where the Ladies' Mile was one of the sights of Europe. Here the fashionable mid-Victorians rode the best-looking hacks they could afford to keep, and were *de rigeur* dressed in black morning coats and beautifully fitted dark blue or black overalls strapped down over highly polished Wellington boots with silver box spurs. The ladies, and some of the older men, were followed at a respectful distance by a groom, dressed in livery with a high hat and cockade. The ladies who did not care to ride were driven up and down in their carriages. The Princess of Wales often appeared, in the morning in a victoria or some light type of carriage, in the evening in a splendidly turned-out barouche.

Lord Ernest Hamilton also left a description of some of the servants who were needed to staff Chesterfield House.

"The master of the internal ceremonies, either in town and country, in the days of my early boy-hood, was a superb functionary of the name of Burgh, known to us and to the neighbouring tradesmen as the "house steward". Burgh was a great man both in stature and in importance. He always wore the short frock-coat of the day, unbuttoned, and the natural majesty of his appearance was enhanced by a pointed grey "imperial". The greater part of Burgh's activities – always a little mysterious to my enquiring mind – were carried on underground but, now and again, he would come to the surface, like a large, prosperous rabbit, and be met with in the passages or on the stair. When this happened, I would say, "Good morning, Burgh," rather tremulously, to which the great man would reply, flattening his considerable bulk against the wall, "Your most obedient, my lord."

THE END OF AN EVENING
Departing guests are shown to their carriages by liveried footmen after a fashionable London party. (*Illustrated London News,* 1847.)

The house steward, sometimes known as the butler, made infrequent appearances in public, but was present occasionally at large dinner parties to pour out the wine. The liaison officer between him and the family was the groom of the chambers, below whom there was an under-butler and a posse of large, imposing footmen. "The footmen, in London, were plush-breeked, silk stockinged, and powdered. In the country they were allowed to dispense with the powder and to wear trousers with a crimson cord down the seam and waistcoats of the family livery. On the rare occasions of big dinner-parties at Chesterfield House, the dark breeches and stockings that did duty for family gatherings were replaced by uniforms of an almost pantomimic splendour – pink poplin breeches and tunics, with huge silver epaulettes and silver aiguilettes dangling down in front."

In great houses such as Chesterfield House there would be a sharp distinction between the upper servants and the under servants, who would even eat separately. The house steward, who kept the household accounts, paid the wages, engaged the menservants and did much of the ordering, would preside over the "second table" (the "first table" was that in his master's dining room). If there was not a steward then the housekeeper occupied the position. The *chef*, the butler, the valet, the groom of the chambers (whose responsibility was the care of the furniture), and the lady's maid were all members of the second table, and took their meals in the steward's room or the housekeeper's room, and were waited on by one of the under-servants. They sat at table in order of precedence according to the importance of their function – the social hierarchy in the servants' hall was as rigidly organized as the rest of the Victorian class system. Visiting servants also had to observe a rule of precedence, only here it was according to their master or their mistress's rank.

The footmen (who would be ranked as under-servants) perhaps deserve a special mention. The prestige of their employers depended upon their appearance and their numbers, and so in novels we often come across the host who has hastily dragged in some uncouth outdoor servants, and pushed them into ill-fitting livery so that he can dazzle his guests. Footmen were engaged mainly on their appearance, their height and the shape of their calves (so important in a silk stocking). Their morals therefore, as Lord Ernest Hamilton commented, left much to be desired, as did their drinking habits. In his experience, the footmen of Chesterfield House were nearly always drunk.

Surtees describes how matters were ordered at Jawleyford Grange. Mr. Jawleyford considered it essential to his position in society that he should be able to display a butler and two footmen, though it might mean dressing a man up at short notice.

"Mr. Jawleyford started life with two most unimpeachable Johns. They were nearly six feet high, heads well up, and legs that might have done for models for a sculptor. They powdered with the greatest propriety, and by two o'clock each day were silk-stockinged and pumped in full Jawleyford livery; sky-blue coats with massive silver aiguillettes, and broad silver seams down the front and round their waistcoat-pocket flaps; silver garters at their crimson plush breeches' knees; and thus attired, they were ready to turn out with the butler to receive visitors, and conduct them back to their carriages. Gradually they came down in style, but not in number, and, when Mr. Sponge visited Mr. Jawleyford, he had a sort of out-of-door man-of-all-work who metamorphosed himself into a second footman at short notice."

After this diversion to scrutinize some of the servants, we must return to the masters. By 1870 London fashionable society had changed. In the earlier years of Victoria's reign it had been small, powerful, and closely connected with government and political power. There had been an element of responsibility about it. But in the later years the range of smart society vastly expanded. There were quantities of rich, well-dressed, idle people, who did not need to be members of a landowning family to be acceptable. "An infectious orgy of idleness and frivolity," wrote a mid-Victorian, remembering the years between 1865 and 1885.

Trollope in *The Way We Live Now* has left a savage account of this era. He shows an irresponsible society, in which everybody is frenziedly pursuing pleasure and riches. The career of the central character, Melmotte, is based on that of Hudson the railway king. Nobody knows where he has come from, nor how he gets his wealth. He appears to be rich, he is lavish with the money he is supposed to have, and society prostrates itself, adoring, before him. He plans to give a great banquet to which the Emperor of China is invited. Invitations for this party are openly bought and sold, everybody with any claim to be smart feels he must be there. And then, just a day or so before the party there are uneasy rumours that Melmotte may be arrested for forgery. Nobody has troubled before this to wonder how he has come by his money; they do not care whether or not he is financially honest; but a police case – that is petty and degrading and quite another matter. And Society stays away from Mr. Melmotte's great reception.

In this same novel Trollope shows us another aspect of the smart London scene – the marriage market. The disposing of a daughter in marriage was one of the important reasons for the yearly move to London, and one of the factors to be taken into consideration when a financially embarrassed landowner wondered if he could afford the expense of keeping on his London house. A girl, it was felt, had absolutely no chance in the country. She would never meet the right sort of man. In *The Way We Live Now* Georgiana Longestaffe is thrown into despairing fury when her father announces that he cannot afford to take his family to London any longer. How can she possibly find a husband now? "What is to become of me? Is it not enough to drive me mad to be going about here by myself, without any prospect of anything? Should you have liked at my age to have felt that you had no chance of having a house of your own to live in?" In the end in her desperation she runs away with the curate – the proud Georgiana who had so despised her sister for stooping to marry a neighbouring squire.

The more regular alliances were usually negotiated by the mothers. The marriages were not arranged in the sense that the French nobility "arranged" theirs. But suggestions might be made, and then the young women would enter the arena and aim for the chosen young men. Ideally, he should be the wealthy heir of a landed family; a younger son, however well-connected, was undesirable because of his poor prospects and lack of income. "The Lady Isabella, and the Lady Augusta . . . each had knocked down her earl. . . . They had played their popular parts without a single blunder. Always in the best set, never flirting with the wrong man, and never speaking to the wrong woman, all agreed that the Ladies St. Maurice had fairly won their coronets."

Disraeli here, in *The Young Duke*, is describing how two young women have made aristocratic alliances. But the Victorian novelist also loved to dwell on the financial alliance, when the heir to an impoverished aristocratic family is told that he must "marry money" and restore the family fortunes with his wife's dowry. Or the poor but well-connected girl realizes that if she is to continue to enjoy the sort of life that she has hitherto taken for

THE DEBUTANTE AND HER MOTHER
Illustrated London News, 1847.

granted, she must accept a wealthy man even though he is dull, and turn her back on the fascinating penniless barrister for whom her heart yearns.

In *The Way We Live Now* Trollope presents Sir Felix Carbury, the vicious, dissolute son of the widowed Lady Carbury, who has run through all his own money as well as his mother's. He knows that the only way out of his difficulties is to marry an heiress, and his mother instructs him to try for Miss Melmotte, the daughter of the shady financier. "Such a man may be ruined at any time; but there was no doubt that to any one marrying his daughter during the present season of his outrageous prosperity he could give a very large fortune indeed." The novel was published in 1875, and Trollope's savage emphasis was on the way we live *now* – the days of aristocratic alliances are over, the fashionable world is dominated by shameless greed for money.

Smart London society was to become increasingly opulent, showy, and vulgar, and by the end of Queen Victoria's reign it was open to anybody who could afford to keep up a position in it. For this the influence of the Prince of Wales, later Edward VII, "this utterly commonplace person", with his taste for the loud, the vulgar, and the rich, may be partly held responsible. We read much of the Gaiety Theatre in the memoirs of the period. The "mashers" were to be seen at the Gaiety, the young men-about-town who had succeeded the drooping and drawling "dandies" of the 60's and 70's. They devoted themselves to the Gaiety girls – Kate Vaughan, Nellie Farren, and their contemporaries – many of whom were to marry into the aristocracy in the 1890's. These young men were also known as the "Crutch and Toothpick Brigade", because it was the fashion to carry smart walking sticks with crutch handles, and to chew toothpicks.

In the 1880's London society took up the "aesthetic revival". Intellectual society had already come under the influence some time before of the pre-Raphaelite painters such as Millais and Burne-Jones, of Ruskin's writings on art, and William Morris's views on design and decoration. But the real impact on fashionable society was made by Oscar Wilde, who came down from Oxford in 1878, and was to be seen drooping at smart London gatherings, with long hair, a flowing tie, and a lily or a sunflower in his hand. Thereupon it became all the rage to look as much like a lily as nature allowed you, and to wander round the Grosvenor Gallery dwelling yearningly on the pre-Raphaelite pictures there. Gilbert and Sullivan's *Patience* guyed the aesthetics in the persons of Bunthorne the "fleshly poet" (supposedly Swinburne) and Archibald Grosvenor the apostle of Simplicity (aimed at Wilde):

> "A pallid and thin young man
> A haggard and lank young man,
> A greenery-yallery, Grosvenor Gallery,
> Foot-in-the-grave young man."

And the dress and make-up of the twenty maidens all consumed with love for Bunthorne were copied from a picture by Burne-Jones.

Disraeli and Trollope are the greatest of the English novelists who showed the life of Victorian high society. During his later years Disraeli knew it from the inside. He mingled with the great at their country house

RIDING IN HYDE PARK
Engraving by Doré (*London*, 1872).

parties and their London receptions. He sat in the House of Commons and had all the gossip of political and fashionable life at his fingertips. But he had been an outsider once. In his early years he had hovered on the fringes of the great world, peering at it longingly. From those days date his early novels, such as *Vivian Grey* and *The Young Duke*. His imagination was vivid and his literary style extravagant and he was later to be bitterly ashamed of his youthful ideas about how fashionable society behaved. He describes, for instance, a young duke who for a whim builds an Alhambra-like palace in Regent's Park, gives a banquet where the tables flow with streams of rosewater while the host wanders among his guests idly scattering sapphires and diamonds. "The life of this gallant was an ocean of enjoyment, and each hour, like each wave, threw up its pearl. How dull was the ball in which he did not bound! How dim the banquet in which he did not glitter! His presence in the Gardens compensated for the want of flowers, his vision in the Park, for the want of sun. In public breakfasts, he was more indispensible than pine-apples; in private concerts more noticed than an absent singer. How fair was the dame on whom he smiled! How brown was the tradesman on whom he frowned!"

Even in Disraeli's more mature novels high society is shown glittering and sparkling; for him the romance of aristocracy never wore off. There were two sides to him; he was capable of writing satirically about certain types of Whig noblemen, but his aristocratic young heroes such as Coningsby, Lothair, and Charles Egremont are altogether different. Graceful, ardent, full of fire and passion, they seem creatures from another world, quite incompatible with the beefy, stolid, sporting young men whom Taine observed when he visited England.

Trollope's world is closer to what Taine found. In his novels we see the solid, apparently secure world of the mid-Victorian landed classes. Their interests are their estates, possibly politics, their problems the unsatisfactory behaviour of their heirs, and how to dispose of their daughters in marriage. They pass two months of the year in their London houses, during which they spend a great deal of time in their clubs while their females do the rounds of the fashionable London entertainments. In the country they give rather dull dinner parties to their neighbours, and play a conscientious, responsible part in the community about them. It is a society that seems so safe, secure, and basically cheerful that many readers are tempted to forget that Trollope, outside the six Barsetshire novels, could write with deep pessimism. In *The Way We Live Now* and *The Eustace Diamonds* he portrayed with savage dislike a smart, fashionable society that had lost all proper sense of values.

There were many romances of high life in the 19th century, by authors who, like the young Disraeli, longed to be part of that charmed circle. Known as "silver fork" novels, they are sometimes tedious, and sometimes so extravagant as to be ludicrous. Ouida's[1] novelettes are written with wild fancifulness and can be very amusing. Ouida was bold and fearless, with great faith in her powers of imagination. She did not hesitate to describe in the first person what it felt like to row in the University boat race, to charge with the Light Brigade, or to gallop cross-country after a famous pack of fox-hounds. Her characters are often shown lounging languidly at smart resorts on the French Riviera, or making weary comments on the smart world as they loll in rooms furnished with fantastic luxury. Their conversation is sprinkled with French phrases and Latin and Greek tags (usually grotesquely wrong). And yet her writing at the time was considered wicked and daring.

Perhaps the most charming of all the "silver fork" writers was the nine-year-old Daisy Ashford whose *The Young Visiters* was first published in 1919, but written considerably earlier. It describes how Mr. Salteena, "an elderly man of 42", goes to London to be made "more like a gentleman", and is introduced into high society. Wearing his host's second best cocked hat, with a silver paper star pinned on his chest he goes to a reception at Buckingham Palace. ("Mr. Salteena purspired rarther hard and gave a hitch to his garters to make sure."). He is received cordially by the Prince of Wales, and although he does not in the end marry the girl he loves, he does find a job "galloping madly after the Royal Carrage in a smart suit of green velvit with knickbockers compleat." *The Young Visiters*, which was strongly influenced by its author's furtive reading of Victorian society novels, is no more fantastic than these, and a great deal more amusing.

1 Ouida (Marie Louise de la Ramée), (1839–1908). Author of forty-five novels, mostly depicting fashionable life as she imagined it.

5 · Squire and Cottager

THE factory age not only brought an increased population, it also altered the pattern of society. Men and their families crowded into the towns, and in the towns they did not find the father-child relationship between employer and labourer that existed in the country, where the squire traditionally had made himself responsible for those who lived and worked on his land. The Victorians themselves realized that this was a way of life that was departing, and they mourned it, for to many it was an ideal way – the landowner, the farmer and the cottager all concerned with the land and the crops that it bore; all worshipping in the same church on Sundays; the landowner keeping a fatherly eye on the needs of his tenants, admonishing, rewarding, and helping where necessary. So perfect and so right did this relationship seem that some Victorians tried to found industrial communities on the same principles. Many, Disraeli among them, could think of no other satisfactory way of dealing with the problems of town life.

There was great confusion among the Victorians about how much should be done for the labouring classes. Dickens and people like him grew heated when they saw the sufferings of the poor ignored by the prosperous, but they were equally enraged by much of the legislation which tried to improve the lot of the sufferers, and by official enquiries into their misery.

Chapter heading from *The Children's Prize*, 1867.

The first they denounced as inhumanity, the second as meddlesome inter-ference with the liberty of the individual. The squire-cottager relationship might sound all very well when considered in the abstract, but despotism when applied to individuals. And despotism was how many of the cottagers regarded it.

Lady Lufton, wrote Trollope in *Framley Parsonage* "desired that all the farmers round her should be able to pay their rents without trouble, that all the old women should have warm flannel petticoats, that the working men should be saved from rheumatism by healthy food and dry houses, that they should all be obedient to their pastors and masters – temporal as well as spiritual. That was her way of loving her country. She desired also that the copses should be full of pheasants, the stubble-field of part-ridges, and gorse covers of foxes; in that way, also she loved her country."

Trollope here has neatly summarized the philosophy of the conscientious smaller Victorian landowner. Lady Lufton might seem of little account beside such landowners as the Duke of Omnium in the same novel, but her powers in her part of Barsetshire are absolute. She is patron of the living and thus able to appoint whatever clergyman she chooses to the parish; as patron and as lady of the manor she feels no hesitation in commenting on the said clergyman's behaviour, and expressing herself as outraged when he visits the Duke of Omnium at Gatherum Castle. Over the village school, too, she exerts strong control. She wishes to appoint one of her protegées as schoolmistress, the vicar wishes to appoint a trained teacher. Lady Lufton wins, for the vicar remarks, " 'If I persist this time, I shall certainly have to yield the next; and then the next may probably be more important.' "

Lady Lufton was no more autocratic than hundreds of others of her kind who sincerely believed that it was upon them and them alone that devolved the duty of supervising the physical and spiritual well-being of the cottagers on their estates. The country squire – "squire" being the colloquial term for the principal landowner of a district – would expect by virtue of his position to be a magistrate and a member of the local Board of Guardians (the body responsible after 1834 for the welfare of the poor of the district). This would have nothing to do with his suitability for the work involved. In Trollope's *Sir Harry Hotspur* the Sir Harry of the title suggests to his disreputable and unreliable young cousin that he should settle down on a small country estate and cool his heels for a few months, and as a further sobering measure "we'll get you made a magistrate for the county." The larger landowner might be lord lieutenant of the county and command the local militia; every squire would be expected to support the affairs of the parish church. They might perform this last duty in a rather tepid fashion, simply by attending the Sunday services, and seeing to it that the servants did as well. Or they might have embarrassingly decided opinions of their own, like the squire whom the diarist Kilvert[1] mentions, who was so zealous in Kilvert's father's parish, taking a fierce line about the church music, and striding into the village school and flinging open all the windows. The squire's wife had her duties too, and would occupy herself with the village school, the local charities, and such matters as the clothing club and savings bank.

Few of the Victorian upper classes queried the fitness of the arrangement whereby the landowner made himself responsible for the lives of the people who worked on his estate. They recognized of course that there were good landowners and bad ones. The bad landlord was concerned to get as high an income as he could from his estates, and to shirk repairs and improvements.

" 'Well, but my dear,' " says Mrs. Jawleyford to her husband in Surtees' novel *Mr. Sponge's Sporting Tour*, " 'you've nothing to do but to tell Mr. Screwemtight to get you some money from the tenants.'

'Money from the tenants!' replied Mr. Jawleyford. 'Screwemtight tells me he can't get another farthing from any man on the estate.'

'Oh, pooh!' said Mrs. Jawleyford; 'you're far too good to them. I always say Screwemtight looks far more to their interest than he does to yours.'

Jawleyford, we may observe, was one of the rather numerous race of paper-booted, pen-and-ink landowners. He always dressed in the country as he would in St. James's Street, and his communications with his tenantry were chiefly confined to dining with them twice a year in the great entrance-hall, after Mr. Screwemtight had eased them of their cash in the steward's room. Then Mr. Jawleyford would shine forth the very impersonification of what a landlord ought to be. Dressed in the height of fashion, as if by his clothes to give the lie to his words, he would expatiate on the delights

1 The Rev. Robert Francis Kilvert (1840–79). Curate of Clyro in Radnorshire for seven years and later vicar of Bredwardine. His diaries (1870–9) give one of the best contemporary accounts of country life.

AN EARLY VICTORIAN LANDOWNER DINING WITH HIS TENANTS
John Leech's drawing of Mr. Jawleyford from *Mr. Sponge's Sporting Tour,* 1853.

of such meetings of equality; declare that, next to those spent with his family, the only really happy moments of his life were those when he was surrounded by his tenantry; he doated on the manly character of the English farmer."

The good landowner was the one who kept his property in good order, repaired the farms and cottages on his estate, was ready to remit rents when times were bad, and who extended a helping hand to the poor man in times of trouble. He would provide employment for the cottager and his children, and material comforts for the needy, interest himself in church matters and the schools of the parish. The good landowner behaved like a benevolent father to all who lived on his estates, and this, it was generally felt among the upper classes, was how it should be, and this was the root of the troubles of the industrial workers. Huddled together in towns, working for masters who were indifferent to their employees, they had no one to keep a watchful, paternal eye on them.

Richard Jefferies[1] in a collection of essays called *Hodge and his Master* published in 1880 praised the large landowner, taking as his example the Earls Bathurst, and the territory that they ruled in Gloucestershire. He disguises the area as "Fleeceborough", but it is in fact Cirencester.

"A peer only at Westminster, here he is a prince, whose dominions are almost co-extensive with the horizon; and this, the capital city, is for the most part his.

Far away stretches that little kingdom, with its minor towns of villages, hamlets and farms. Broad green meadows, where the cattle graze beside the streams and in the plains; rolling uplands, ploughed and sown, where the barley flourishes; high hills and shadowy woods; grey church towers; new glaring schools; quiet wayside inns, and ancient farmhouses tenanted for generations by the same families."

Richard Jefferies spoke of the benefits of renting land from a very large

THE HEIR'S COMING-OF-AGE FESTIVITIES AT
BURGHLEY HOUSE, 1846

The Marchioness of Exeter, her son standing beside her, receiving children from the local village schools. The *Illustrated London News* commented: "All were bidden to the feast who were in the most remote degree connected with the estate; and the poor of the district were furnished with the means of being glad, as well as their neighbours in better circumstances."

1 Richard Jefferies (1848–87). Naturalist and writer. Son of a Wiltshire farmer, he first attracted notice with his *Gamekeeper at Home* (1878). Besides studies of country life he also wrote less successful novels and an autobiography.

owner, who was able to be more liberal in the way of repairs and improvements, and had the resources to support losses which would press heavily
upon the small owner. Such an owner, Jefferies said rapturously, would
never interfere and would leave his tenants personally free. Then, somewhat contradicting himself, he speaks of the all-pervading influence of
the owners of "Fleeceborough".

"Occasionally mysterious allusions are made to 'he', what 'he' will do
with a certain farm, whether 'he' will support such and such a movement,
or subscribe to some particular fund, what view will 'he' take on the local
question of the day? . . . 'He' is the resident within those vast and endless
walls, with the metal gates and the gilded coronet above – the prince of
this kingdom and its capital city.

No matter what subject is to the front, the question is always heard –
What will 'he' do? What will 'he' say to it? The Volunteers compete for
prizes which 'he' offers. The cottage hospital; the flower show; the cattle
show, or agricultural exhibition; the new market buildings arose through
his subscription and influence; the artesian well, sunk that the town might
have the best of water, was bored at his expense; and so on, through the
whole list of town affairs."

"What manner of man is this 'despot' and prince behind his vast walls?"
Jefferies asks. His answer is that it matters little. The family has always
chosen to stay in the background, never obtruding their presence, but
ruling their kingdom with humanity, wisdom, and generosity. "His
predecessors did it, he does it, and the next to come will do it. It is the tradition of the house."

This, to Jefferies, and to thousands of others of his time, seemed an ideal
state of affairs. But the cottager was not always so contented, although–
uneducated and inarticulate – he was rarely able to express his feelings on
the subject. In a pamphlet of 1893 addressed to farm labourers, an adherent
of the English Land Restoration League set down his resentment at the
way a landowner, however benevolent he might seem to the outside world,
dominated the lives of those who worked on his estates. In the parish of
Stanton St. Bernard in Wiltshire, the Earl of Pembroke owned some
2,000 acres of land, which he rented to two farmers.

"The two farmers, besides controlling the cultivation of all the land in the parish, and the tenancy of all the cottages, are the churchwardens, and overseers of the poor and the school managers. One of them has charge of the rate books. Nothing could well be simpler than this system of parish government. The labourer who wants to work in the parish must obtain employment on the Earl of Pembroke's land under one of the Earl of Pembroke's two farmers, who will house him in one of the Earl's cottages, deducting the rent from his weekly wages. He sends his children to the 'national' school (managed by the Earl of Pembroke's farmers), and goes on Sunday to the Church where, under the eyes of the two churchwardens (Lord Pembroke's farmers again), he 'sits under' a clergyman appointed to the parish (by the Earl of Pembroke). When he gets too old to work, or is reduced to hopeless poverty by misfortune, he must apply for Poor Law relief to the same two farmers. If, in spite of all these arrangements for his comfort, he is still discontented with his lot, there is no building – not even a schoolroom which is largely subsidized out of the taxes – in which he can meet to take counsel with his fellows, unless he first obtains the permission of the Earl of Pembroke's farmers. If the parish of Stanton St. Bernard were a slave estate, owned by the Earl of Pembroke and managed by two overseers on the Earl's behalf, the condition of the inhabitants could hardly be more completely one of slavery than it is today.''

From this it will be seen that the farmers were as much resented as the landowners. The Victorian farmer, for the most part, farmed land that was not his own but was rented from the landowner. The same family might have stayed in that particular farm for generations, the lease renewed time and time again, for the landowner would be as anxious to keep a good tenant as the farmer to stay on the land where his father, his grandfather, and his great-grandfather had worked before him. But the farmer had changed his social habits a great deal during the course of the 19th century.

At the beginning of the century farmers as a class were still men who worked with their hands, beside the men whom they employed. Their sons might well have gone to the same dame schools as the agricultural labourers' children, and when they grew old enough would have worked on the land with their fathers. The farmer's wife was likely to be a bustling sort of body who concerned herself with the poultry yard and the dairy and worked as hard as any of her maids. George Eliot's account of the Poysers' farm in *Adam Bede*, although it refers to 1799, describes a type of

THE FARMER IN HIS FIELDS
Illustration from *The Infant's Magazine*, 1868.

farming family that certainly was common during the first fifty years of the next century.[1] The Poysers live in a fine old house, where the front rooms are unused; life radiates not from the parlour but from the kitchen and the farmyard. The old Martin Poyser who now sits dozing by the fire has yielded the farm to his son, Martin the younger, a burly, slow-moving, red-faced man who is moved to wrath only when he spots incompetent farming on neighbouring land. The farm-servants, outdoor and indoor, live on the farm and eat in the kitchen with the Poyser family. The kitchen gleams with pewter and oak, the polishing of which Mrs. Poyser supervises with a vigilant eye. When we first meet her she is ironing, but keenly watching the activities of her niece who is in the dairy making up the butter, and of the maid who is baking. There are no airs about the Poysers. When they go along with everybody else on the estate to the birthday celebrations of the squire's grandson, they make their way in a covered cart together with the farm servants. "The fuller the cart the better, because then the

1 Taine was assured by English friends that George Eliot's portrait of the Poysers was strikingly true to life.

jolting would not hurt so much and [the dairymaid's] broad person and thick arms were an excellent cushion to be pitched on."

Jefferies, in 1880, wrote of the wide-spread social changes that had appeared in the country by that time. There was now a new breed, the gentle-man farmer, who knew little or nothing about farming, but liked country life. He was essentially a business man, he grudged the money required to buy a thousand acres; as a tenant farmer he could keep his capital, and be free to give up the life at will. A bailiff ran the farm for him, the gentleman farmer merely kept an eye on the accounts. He lived in a newly-built mansion furnished in the latest style, glittering with ormolu and cut-glass prisms and richly upholstered. Friends came down to the shooting, hunting and fishing, the family travelled to the Continent, and the wife and daughters, elegantly dressed, drove round the country lanes in a carriage with silver-plated harness and a liveried coachman.

The old style of farmer, the Martin Poyser sort in his antique breeches and gaiters that used to be seen in the local town on market day fumbling in the bottom of his canvas bag for silver and gold, was no longer to be found. The farmer's wife who with her daughters had attended to her poultry, geese and turkeys, who had made the butter and cheese and helped salt the bacon, – she was a fine lady now with kid gloves on her hands, who moved in a rustle of silk and satin and a waving of ostrich feathers. The daughter was pale and interesting, she played Beethoven and painted, the son rode to hounds, and expensive hired help attended to the poultry and the dairy.

The civilization of the town, said Jefferies, had taken root in the country, and he argued that the old spirit of earnest work and prudence had gone from the farmer. The women in their town clothes could not tuck up their sleeves and see to the butter or feed the poultry. It had made a great difference to country society. Before, everybody had worked personally with his hands. Now there was a distinct social barrier between those who laboured and those who did not. There was also the question of economics. This new gentility was the downfall of the small farm, he thought. The small farm needed thrift and steady hard work to be profitable, and could not support the mistress and the misses playing the fine lady. To this new type of farmer he attributed much of the ill that had befallen English agriculture in the latter half of the century.

The years which, according to Jefferies, had seen the creeping of a town civilization across the face of agricultural England had also seen a great improvement in the farming. Throughout the '40's, '50's and '60's new methods of cultivation, draining, fertilising, and new machines replaced the conservative, centuries-old methods of Martin Poyser and his kind; the golden age of British agriculture was reckoned to be the ten years between 1853 and 1862. But a series of bad harvests in the 1870's culminated in the disastrous year of 1879 when one of the worst harvests of the century combined with outbreaks of cattle and sheep disease. Farmers were unable to pay their rents, and the income of landlords, tenants and labourers fell heavily. The import of cheap corn from America and tinned and frozen meat affected the prices at home, and though the town population benefited from the cheap new food, the English food producers suffered. The big landlords still had the resources behind them to stem back disaster, they remitted rents, and a series of good harvests in the '80's enabled them to balance their accounts. But it was at the cost of neglecting improvement of the land, and a second depression in the '90's found the agricultural community with nothing to draw upon. Many landlords were ruined, their farmers could not pay the rents, they could not find tenants for the farms, and thousands of workers were driven from the land to find work in towns.

P. Anderson Graham, wrote in *The Rural Exodus* (1892) of a visit to Norfolk, one of the most properous wheat-growing areas of England, where he drove through mile after mile of uncultivated country – the landowners being unable to find tenants for the farms. These great losses and dwindling incomes impoverished the landed gentry. The might of the aristocrats who relied on rents from their land dwindled still further, as has been described in chapter three. The splendour of their style of living was reduced, and many of them went abroad to live more cheaply – there are plenty of references in novels of the period to the landowner who takes his family to some place as Baden Baden or Pau while he lets the family home to a wealthy business man.

And the agricultural labourer – "Hodge" as he was called with a kind of pitying contempt – what of him? He was throughout the century one of the most down-trodden workers in the community, ill-housed, ill-paid, half-starved, illiterate, and deprived even of the sympathetic attention that the city slum-dweller received from journalists, novelists and philanthropists. The intense poverty of the agricultural labourer did not obtrude

THE LABOURER'S COTTAGE AS IMAGINED BY A VICTORIAN
ILLUSTRATOR

From *Hymns in Prose*, 1863.

itself in the same way, country life was thought to be pleasanter and healthier, and the man himself was far less articulate than his city equivalent. Acute observers of the miseries of the city poor were deceived by the rose-wreathed cottage that they saw in the country into thinking that the lot of the agricultural poor, if not idyllic, was at least fairly comfortable. In *The Old Curiosity Shop* Dickens brings Nell and her grandfather, after their nightmare journey through the Black Country where he has described the desolation, the terror and the famine that an industrial civilization has brought to the countryside, to the haven of a small country village where in contrast all is peace and serenity.

"They admired everything – the old grey porch, the mullioned windows, the venerable gravestones dotting the green churchyard, the ancient tower, the very weathercock; the brown thatched roofs of cottage, barn, and homestead, peeping from among the trees; the stream that rippled by the distant watermill; the blue Welsh mountains far away. It was for such a spot the child had wearied in the dense, miserable haunts of labour. Upon her bed of ashes, and amidst the squalid horrors through which they had forced their way, vision of such scenes – beautiful indeed, but not more beautiful than this sweet reality – had always been present to her mind."

"This sweet reality" was as likely as not a community of half-starved labourers living in clay-floored, derelict hovels, but Dickens for all his contempt for those who could not grasp the realities of poverty was himself here dazzled by the picturesqueness of the scene into thinking that the lives of those cottagers under "the brown thatched roofs" were picturesque too.

Francis George Heath, an observer of British rural life, ruefully describes how easy it was to be deceived on this score. In 1873, on a tour of the West Country, he came upon a charming hamlet. A brook ran in front of a row of creeper-grown cottages; the gardens had beehives in them, fruit trees and vegetables; orchards grew round about. It seemed on first sight to be a rural paradise. But when he investigated the life of one of the families that inhabited this Arcady, he found terrifying misery. The husband was a carter earning ten shillings a week, 8s. 7d. when all deductions for rent and rates were made – on which to support eight people. There was hardly any furniture, the glass was out of the windows, the roof

THE COTTAGER ENVIES HIS LANDLORD'S PIGS
Standing in front of his derelict cottage, the farm labourer contrasts this with the
comfort of the pigsty. (*Punch*, 1863.)

leaked. Seven people slept in one room, four in the only bed, three on the
floor. There was an old bed-ridden grandmother who received three
shillings a week from the parish. The family was hopelessly in debt, they
were rearing a pig, but most of it when it was killed would have to go to
meet the bills they had incurred while feeding it, and if the pig should die
their prospects were appalling.

The agricultural labourer was not a romantic figure. He was seen, even
by a sympathetic onlooker, as a shambling, slouching, boorish, degraded
creature, improvident, reckless, and always on the watch for what he
could get out of the gentry. Charles Kingsley[1] in *Yeast*, the one notable
novel that was written during the 19th century about the plight of the agricultural poor, makes his young hero Lancelot blench at the sight of the

[1] Charles Kingsley (1819–75). Writer and churchman. Took much interest in social
reform, and contributed to the *Christian Socialist*. His numerous writings include children's books such as *The Water Babies*, as well as novels, poetry, and sermons.

revellers at the village fair. He had hoped to see perhaps Maypole dancing and games. What he found was drunkenness and foul language, under-sized and under-fed youths and girls with degenerate feature. But above all he is appalled by the way they speak. He cannot even understand their conversation.

"It was half articulate, nasal, guttural, made up almost entirely of vowels, like the speech of savages. He had never before been struck with the signi-ficant contrast between the sharp, clearly defined articulation, the vivid and varied tones of the gentleman, or even of the London street-boy when compared with the coarse, half-formed growls, as of a company of seals, which he heard round him."

The young gamekeeper who has taken Lancelot to the fair gives him reasons for the degradation that so repels him. The degenerate physical appearance of the young people compared to their parents is due to bad food, bad housing, bad nursing in the years that followed the Napoleonic Wars. The foul language of the women is due to the fact that from early childhood they have been employed in the fields. " 'It wears them out in body, sir, that fieldwork,' " says the gamekeeper to Lancelot, " 'and makes them brutes in soul and in manners,. " He explains too that the well-meaning benevolence of the better sort of gentry has degraded the labourer and made him whining, canting and deceitful, ready to screw all he can from the charitable. Of a local landowner he says:

" 'But, sir, as sure as you live he's making his people slaves and humbugs. He doesn't see, sir, that they want to be raised bodily out of this miserable hand-to-mouth state, to be brought nearer up to him, and set on a footing where they can shift for themselves. Without meaning it, sir, all his bound-less charities are keeping the people down, and telling them they must stay down, and not help themselves, but wait for what he gives them. He fats prize-labourers, sir, just as Lord Minchampstead fats prize-oxen and pigs.' "

The history of the agricultural labourer in the 19th century makes sad reading. Conditions varied from district to district and were better in the north where the working man seems always to have been sturdier, more

self-reliant, and altogether tougher. But everywhere the employers appear to have exercised a cruel mastery over labour, sometimes claiming the work of the entire family at a very low wage. Children were often forced to work with their fathers at six years old or less, and should an older boy leave, the employer might well give the father notice on the grounds that the family was not large enough to do the work. By 1880 education was compulsory from the age of five for every child, but employers found it fairly easy to evade the law to take the boy they wanted from school – and parents were glad enough of the few extra shillings that it brought in.

Wages varied according to the locality, but except in the north, they were barely enough to support a man and his family, and often less than enough. There was extra at harvest time; there were perquisites like free beer, and the gleanings from the harvest fields, but still the cottager might be so hungry that he would steal turnips from the fields. The townsman's idea of the cottager living off the produce of his own land was not often borne out by fact. Many cottages were without gardens; Enclosure Acts had taken the land where the labourer might have grazed his animals or cultivated a strip, and many farmers refused the men allotments, saying they needed all the land for themselves, or else they rented out portions of land at a price far above that which they paid themselves. It was a commonplace for them to forbid the labourer to keep a pig or fowls, on the grounds that the man might be tempted to steal grain to feed it. Pheasants, partridges, hares – all these were game, the property of the landowner, and the penalties for poaching them were severe. But even the rabbit that ran across the fields where the labourer was working might not be touched, nor might he pick up an injured or a dead one and take it home. Rabbits were vermin and a pest, but still the poor man was not allowed to eat them. If he found a marauding hare among the young plants in his garden, that hare was the squire's and must not be snared or trapped however much havoc it wrought.

The diet of the labourer was not enough to support the long hours he worked. There was usually a fourteen-hour day, perhaps more, with a long tramp of sometimes four miles to reach his work. In bad weather he would have to spend the day working in drenched clothes – which meant that a great many labourers were early crippled with rheumatism. Canon Girdlestone, who spoke out hotly against the conditions of Devon labourers in the 1860's, reported that in North Devon the men were paid a weekly wage of 7s. 8d. For breakfast they could only afford "tea-kettle-broth" i.e., slices of dry bread with hot water poured over them, perhaps with the addition of an onion or half a teaspoon of milk (though milk was rarely obtainable; the farmers fed any surplus to the pigs.) Lunch consisted of skim-milk cheese, and bread; supper, potatoes and cabbage with (if the labourer was allowed to keep a pig) a tiny piece of bacon. There was meat only on Sundays. Drinking water was fetched from the village brook, or from exposed wells into which oozed the open sewers.

In 1869 an Oxfordshire woman told an investigator: "My husband is a milkman and gets 12s. We pay 1s. 9d. rent, and have only one bed-room. Last week I got 3d. for a bit of sewing, so we had 12s. 3d., and I spent it this way – meat, 3s. 7½d.; bread, 3s.; rent, 1s. 9d.; tea, sugar, flour, soap, and soda, 3s. 7½d.; boys' schooling, 2d.; total, 12s. 2d. So I had a penny left."

She was a fortunate woman. Many cottagers were entangled in debt from which they never struggled free. They owed the village shop money before they ever received their wages; and as Francis Heath observed, if they had a pig very likely they reckoned to pay off the cost of fattening it with part of the price they would get for its meat. If the pig died from swine fever it might be ruin for the whole family.

" 'And there's another mistake in your charitable great people, sir,' " says Kingsley's gamekeeper in *Yeast*. " 'When they see poor folk sick or hungry before their eyes, they pull out their purses fast enough, God bless them; for they wouldn't like to be so themselves. But the oppression that goes on all the year round, and the filth, and the lying, and the swearing, and the profligacy, that go on all the year round, and the sickening weight of debt, and the miserable grinding anxiety from rent-day to rent-day, and Saturday night to Saturday night, that crushes a man's soul down, and drives every thought out of his head but how he is to fill his stomach and warm his back, and keep a house over his head, till he daren't for his life take his thoughts one moment off the meat that perishest – oh, sir, they never felt this; and, therefore, they never dream that there are thousands who pass them in their daily walks who feel this, and feel nothing else.' "

The farm labourers did not share in any of the prosperity enjoyed by the farmers in the middle years of the century. They saw that the man who employed them was sending his sons to be educated at the university, dressing his wife and daughters in fine clothes, buying hunters, while the labourers remained ill-fed, uneducated, housed in hovels where the farmer would have disdained to put his cattle. "Men do not run away in shoals from homes where their childhood was happy," wrote a clergyman commenting on the decay of rural life in the 1880's, and the flood of workers who were leaving the land. "They *do* run away from the odious thoughts of living and dying in a squalid hovel with a clay floor and two dark cabins under the rafters reached by a ricketty ladder, in one of which sleep father and mother as best they can, while in the foetid air of the other their offspring of both sexes huddle, sometimes eight or nine of them, among them young men and young women out of whom you are stamping all sense of shame."

Kingsley's gamekeeper in *Yeast* composed a ballad in which he set down some of the sorrows of the poor cottager. He called it *A Rough Rhyme on a Rough Matter*.

"You have sold the labouring man, squire,
　　Body and soul to shame,
To pay for your seat in the House, squire,
　　And to pay for the feed of your game.

You made him a poacher yourself, squire,
　　When you'd give neither work nor meat;
And your barley-fed hares robbed the garden
　　At our starving children's feet;

When packed in one reeking chamber,
　　Man, maid, mother, and little ones lay;
While the rain pattered in on the rotting bride-bed,
　　And the walls let in the day;

When we lay in the burning fever
　　On the mud of the cold clay floor,
Till you parted us all for three months, squire,
　　At the cursed workhouse door.

We quarrelled like brutes, and who wonders?
　　What self-respect could we keep,
Worse housed than your hacks and your pointers,
　　Worse fed than your hogs and your sheep?"

But more than all these miseries, it seems, the agricultural labourer resented his complete dependence upon the landowner and the farmer – upon the gentry, in fact. As he saw it, they refused to pay him a living wage, but when he was in want doled out small benefits to him if they were of a magnanimous turn of mind – or withheld them if they were not. Either way, the cottager resented it, nor could the benevolent landowner understand his resentment. "He cannot understand that the poor have their ambitions," said Anderson Graham speaking of squires. "Often in talking to a great landed proprietor, who on many points seemed benevolence and good-nature personified. I have seen a cloud come over his brow as soon as I hinted any scheme meant to afford the peasants greater facilities for rising in the world. To a certain passage in the Church Catechism about 'doing my duty in that state of life into which it has pleased God to call me' he attaches quite too much importance."

Anybody who has read the literature for cottagers put out by such pub-

THE STABLE AND THE COTTAGE

Mr. Punch points out to the landowner the contrast between the comfort in which his horse lives, and the misery of his farm workers. (*Punch,* 1861.)

lishers as the Religious Tract Society will recognize the truth of this. There were hundreds of thousands of little stories and homilies published during the Victorian period urging their readers to be thrifty, to adjure smoking and drinking, and to do their duty in that state of life into which it had pleased God to call them. The authors, usually anonymous, pointed out the follies of ambition and the blessings of contentment. The earlier tales were severe on the cottage girl who tried to imitate the dress of the gentry, or to adorn herself in a way unfitting to her class. Such diversions as dancing, it was said, were acceptable for the squire's daughters, but were dangerous for the cottage girl who might be led into low company thereby. Any attempt by the girls at the village school to wear a fringe on their spencers, or too long legs to their pantalettes must be squashed by the ladies who taught there. Nor did the ladies of the village restrict their interference to the children. Juliana Horatia Ewing,[1] the author of some of the best children's books of the century, herself the daughter of a country clergy-man, writes in one of her letters of the trouble she has had in persuading one of her father's parishioners not to trim a hat too gaudily.

In a story by Jean Ingelow[2] (*Studies for Stories*, 1870), we find a village girl who is ambitious to leave home to become a milliner. Probably this would be unwise; a country girl's life in a strange town could well be very wretched. But the vicar who lectures her on her folly makes it seem a sin because she wishes to rise from her station.

"'It is, as you know, a duty to fit ourselves for the station in which it has pleased God to place us. It may be natural, it may be allowable, it may be advantageous, to try to rise from it; but in this case I cannot see the duty. You are placed where you are by Providence, that is to say, your present position has arisen out of circumstances that took place without your will or ordering. . . . You now wish to break away from your place and station, and step into a different sphere. . . . You wish to change your occupation, then you should first have reason to think you are not throwing aside work which Providence has assigned to you and are not rashly making work for yourself which it was never intended you should do.'"

1 Mrs. J. H. Ewing (1841–85), née Gatty. Her books give an excellent account of Vic-torian middle-class childhood.
2 Jean Ingelow (1820–97). Poet. Her works include stories for children as well as three series of poems.

The farm labourer had rarely the wits or the education to speak up for himself. But occasionally in the 19th century we come across a pamphlet which one of them has addressed to his fellows, such as *The Farm Labourer's Catechism* (published in Andover in 1884). It is a parody of the Church of England catechism which formed the basis of the teaching at the village school if it was a church school.

"Q What is your name?

A Clodhopper.

Q Who gave you that name?

A My masters, the landowners and farmers, when I was made a tiller of the soil, a scarer of birds, a snagger of turnips, a keeper of cows and sheep, a follower of the plough, a sower and reaper, a producer of wealth, that my masters might live in idleness and luxuriousness all the days of their lives."

Particularly bitter is the farm labourer's parody of the Apostles' Creed.

"I believe in the landowners and farmers, our kind and generous friends, the authors and conservators of our present condition; in the Labourers' Friend Societies, established for our especial benefit, the promoters every year offering prizes to those of us who beget and rear the greatest number of children, that there may be no lack in the future, of serfs to supply the wants of our masters, and minister to their comfort. I believe it to be to the interest of the landowners and farmers that the tillers of the soil should be kept without the means of education, that they may the more easily keep them in a state of submission to their will and dictates, and regard the formation of School Boards and Secular Education as devices of the 'Evil One'. I believe in the Clergy of the 'Established Church', who in the goodness of their hearts condescend to distribute among us soup, coals, and blankets, bought with money collected at the village Church and supplimented [*sic*] by the toilers pence; the loan of baby-linen when young serfs are born; and for many other mercies received at their hands being truly grateful.

I believe in the Clergy, for they have preached unto us contentment with the station unto which we have been called, it being our duty to bear and suffer, and complain not."

The parody of the ten commandments by the same anonymous author includes injunctions that the labourer will labour for no other than his employer, that he will not listen to agitators who talk about better conditions, that he will not behave disrespectfully, for his employer is on the Bench of Magistrates, and the fifth commandment runs: "Honour the Squire, the landowners, the farmers, the Magistrates, the guardians of the Poor, the bailiff, and the Gamekeeper, that thy days may be long spared to enjoy such blessings."

Though Thomas Hardy wrote of rural characters, and though he described in vivid detail country scenes and farm labour (take, for instance, the pig killing in *Jude the Obscure*, and the threshing scene in *Tess of the D'Urbervilles*), he was primarily interested in the struggles of his characters against the forces of destiny, rather than in their immediate surroundings, so that his books cannot be taken as a representative account of the rural life of his times. But in the picture of Jude Fawley as a boy he conveys memorably the longings of a cottage boy to break away from the land and the hamlet life, and to venture into the outside world which, though physically near, seems hopelessly unattainable. The eleven-year-old Jude has heard of Christminster – Hardy's Oxford – from the schoolmaster. He

FARM LABOURERS IN DORSET, 1846
Illustrated London News.

dreams of it while he stands in the farmer's fields, listlessly whirling his clacker to keep the rooks from the farmer's new-sown fields. Then, finding out the direction in which Christminster lies, he walks up on to the open downs, further from the hamlet than he has ever wandered before. Standing on a barn top, the highest point he can reach, he prays that the haze on the horizon will lift so that he can see this city which, he has been told, is the seat of all learning. And at last the mist clears and he sees light gleaming on the spires and domes of Christminster. From that moment the place becomes for Jude a sacred city.

The man who perhaps did most to help the farm labourer help himself was Joseph Arch who in the 1870's threw himself into organizing Agricultural Labourers' Unions. When he began this work the labourer had no means whatever of voicing his needs. Until 1884 he had no vote; if he agitated for better conditions his overlords, the farmer and the landowner, would probably label him a firebrand and were in a position to make life very difficult for him and his family. Joseph Arch, who was born in 1826, had bitter memories of the despotism of the parson's wife in his childhood. She had strong views about such matters as the way the village schoolgirls should have their hair cut, and the cottage women were obliged to curtsey to her in church as they passed her pew. When he had children of his own, the parson's wife objected to his little daughter wearing a hair net tricked out with white beads that he had bought for her.

But what drove iron into his soul, and turned him into a lifelong rebel against the established order was the sight, at Communion, of the rigid rules of precedence even in the church. "First, up walked the squire to the communion rails; the farmers went up next; then up went the tradesmen, the shopkeepers, the wheelwright and the blacksmith; and then, the very last of all, went the poor agricultural labourers in their smock frocks." He was not alone in resenting this. Joseph Ashby of Tysoe, born a generation later, reported that his mother had been motioned back by the vicar at the communion rail, to make way for a farmer's wife. But she had spoken up and rebuked the vicar in St. Paul's words, telling him that there was no respect of persons with God.

Both Joseph Arch and Joseph Ashby complained of the village schools, where there was far too much emphasis on the catechism, and duty towards one's neighbour. "It was upon this," said Joseph Ashby, "that the Vicar and his lady laid such stress. Boys and girls must never 'pick and steal', nor lie, nor have any envy of folk luckier than themselves; they must learn to labour truly to get their own living and order themselves lowly and reverently to their betters. . . . The word 'betters' was especially firmly underlined and annotated. It meant the Vicar himself and the man who paid your father's wage."

Joseph Arch published his autobiography in 1898. By that time he was a member of Parliament, and the lot of the farm labourer had improved. Farmers had accepted that their workers could belong to a trade union, wages had gone up, there was state education for all, improved living conditions. But by that time vast numbers of workers had left the land and would never return, and town civilization as Jefferies had described it was creeping across agricultural England.

All the changes that have been described in this chapter are to be found in Flora Thompson's trilogy of reminiscences collected together under the title *Lark Rise to Candleford*. Lark Rise is the Oxfordshire hamlet where the narrator Laura (who is in fact Flora Thompson herself) spent her childhood in the 1880's; Candleford the market town near which she went to live and work when she left school. In Lark Rise when she was a child there were people who could remember it in the days before the Enclosure Acts, when it was a wide expanse of open heath. Referring to the opening years of the 19th century Flora Thompson wrote:

"Country people had not been so poor when Sally was a girl, or their prospects so hopeless. Sally's father had kept a cow, geese, pigs, and a donkey-cart to carry his produce to the market town. He could do this because he had commoners' rights and could turn his animals out to graze, and cut furze for firing and even turf to make a lawn for one of his customers. Her mother made butter, for themselves and to sell, baked their own bread, and made candles for lighting."

Seventy years or so later, when Laura is growing up in Lark Rise, affairs are altered very much for the worse. The old independence of the country people that Sally had known as a child has gone. The rough heath that they had used as their own is now divided up into fields which belong to the local landowner, and the men of the hamlet – who in Sally's childhood had been self-supporting – now work for the farmer who rents the land. At 10s. a week it is a struggle, and though everybody has enough to eat (for in this hamlet the cottagers are lucky enough to have gardens and allotments), very often wages are pledged to the shopkeepers in advance, and the women are hard-pushed to clothe their families ("I reckon I'll have to black my backside and go naked" is a familiar joke).

The people that Laura knew, though slow in speech and slow in their ways, were not the down-trodden, whining, feckless "Hodges" that Kingsley had shown thirty years earlier. They had their pride and their independence. Most of the cottages were rented from tradesmen in the local market town, and the inhabitants looked down upon people who lived in cottages belonging to the squire or the farmers, as poor creatures who had no independence. In the 1880's the gentry still lorded it over the cottager.

"At the sight of the squire the people trembled," Joseph Arch had said. "He lorded it right feudally over his tenants, the farmers; the farmers in their turn tyrannized over the labourers; the labourers were no better than

PRIVATE CHARITY COMES TO THE HELP OF THE
STARVING COTTAGER
Illustration from *The Children's Friend*, 1866.

toads under a harrow." Flora Thompson bears this out. Speaking of the lady of the manor – the local squire's mother – she says that she was generous out of all proportion to her small means, she supported two old pen-sioners, gave soup to the "deserving poor", annually entertained the schoolchildren, and fulfilled her duty as she had been taught it in the early years of the century.

"But it would be almost impossible for any one born in this century to imagine the pride and importance of such small country gentlepeople in the 'eighties. As far as was known, the Bracewells were connected with no noble family; they had but little land, kept up but a small establishment, and were said in the village and hamlet to be 'poor as crows'. Yet, by virtue of having been born into a particular caste and of living in the 'big house' of the parish, they expected to reign over their poorer neighbours and to be treated by them with the deference due to royalty. Like royalty, too, they could be charming to those who pleased them. Those who did not had to beware.

A good many of the cottagers still played up to them, the women curtsey-ing to the ground when their carriage passed and speaking in awed tones in their presence. Others ... having breathed the new free air of democracy, which was then beginning to percolate even into such remote places, were inclined to laugh at their pretensions. 'We don't want nothin' from they,' they would say, 'and us shouldn't get it if us did. Let the old gal stay at home and see that her own tea-caddy's kept locked up, not come nosing round here axin' how many spoonsful we puts in ours.'"

But, as Flora Thompson pointed out, the world was changing in the '80's. The vicar might still preach sermons on the supreme rightness of the social order to a congregation arranged in descending orders of rank.

"God, in His infinite wisdom, had appointed a place for every man, woman, and child on this earth and it was their bounden duty to remain contentedly in their niches. A gentleman might seem to some of his listeners to have a pleasant, easy life, compared to theirs at field labour; but he had his duties and responsibilities, which would be far beyond their capabilities. He had to pay taxes, sit on the Bench of Magistrates, oversee his estate, and keep up his position by entertaining. Could they do these things? No.

Of course they could not; and he did not suppose that a gentleman could cut as straight a furrow or mow or thatch a rick as expertly as they could. So let them be thankful and rejoice in their physical strength and the bounty of the farmer, who found them work on his land and paid them wages with his money."

This was the old order, which was on its way out. While Laura is still at the village school, the schoolmistress who had supported the old ways and had taught deference to one's social betters, is replaced by teachers who bring with them the changing spirit of the times, and who tell the children that poor people's souls are as valuable and their minds as capable of culti-vation as those of the rich; who remind them that some boys of poor parents had struck out for themselves and become great men.

But with this new spirit of equality is coming the town civilization that Jefferies laments. The country crafts are disappearing, the householders no longer bake their own bread and brew their own beer, machine-made shoddy objects are replacing the old country-made pieces of furniture, the smocks of the farm men are giving way to mass-produced suits of stiff, dark brown corduroy. In the '90's the market town of Candleford is swallowing up the village of Candleford Green where Laura works, and black-coated, white-collared clerks and shopkeepers are replacing the country-bred inhabitants. Worse still, the farm labourer is now so des-pised and slighted that boys leaving school seek for any job rather than his.

The rural population is pouring into the towns, and the country will soon be occupied in large numbers by the town-dweller who values it for its clean air and open spaces, but who is certainly not prepared to work there.

6 · The Middle Classes

MATTHEW ARNOLD[1] in *Culture and Anarchy*, written in 1869, divided English society into Barbarians, Philistines, and Populace – the aristocracy, the middle class, and the workers. It is easy enough to identify aristocrats and workers; the middle class is more perplexing. It is a class so vast that it has to be sub-divided into classes of its own, and only a specialist can understand the subtleties and shades of these sub-divisions, which range from the upper-middle class – that élite body who were to be the new patricians of England, the class from which Arnold, son of Dr. Thomas Arnold, headmaster of Rugby, was drawn – to the seedy respectability of Mr. Pooter in George Grossmith's *Diary of a Nobody*, the pathetic clerk whose whole life is a struggle to remind the neighbours that he is a gentleman.

Matthew Arnold saw the middle class as the business men, the product of the urban civilization that had been sweeping over England since the beginning of the 19th century – "that great body which, as we know, 'has done all the great things that have been done in all departments'" – ranging

1 Matthew Arnold (1822–88). Poet and critic. Son of Thomas Arnold, the headmaster of Rugby School. A school inspector for over thirty years, he was deeply interested in the improvement of education in England. As well as poetry, he published important essays on literary criticism and on English social and political life.

Chapter heading from *The Infant's Magazine*, 1868.

from the merchant or manufacturer who had risen to be member of Parliament, to the tradesmen. But this is to make too simple a matter of it, and the
one thing that can be said definitely of the class structure in the Victorian
period is that it was not simple.

It was at its simplest in the country. There were even as late as the 1880's,
as Flora Thompson describes in *Lark Rise to Candleford*, two main classes:

A CLERGYMAN VISITING A COTTAGE HOME
Illustration from *The Children's Prize*, 1868.

the cottagers and "the gentry". To the cottagers of Lark Rise, their own life was the normal one. "On one side of that norm were the real poor, living in slums, and, on the other, 'the gentry'. They recognized no other division of classes; although, of course, they knew there were a few 'bettermost people' between. The visiting clergymen and that kind friend of them all, the doctor in the market town, had more money and better houses than theirs, and though they were both 'gentlemen born' they did not belong to the aristocracy inhabiting the great country houses or visiting the hunting boxes around. But these were, indulgently, 'th' ole parson', and, affectionately, 'our doctor'; they were not thought of as belonging to any particular class of society." There was also the village schoolmistress who hovered uneasily between "the bettermost people" and the cottagers. Hers must have been a lonely life, for by her education she was reckoned to be on a higher social level than the agricultural workers, but the gentry certainly did not recognize her as one of themselves. Indeed they were puzzled to know how to treat her socially. Should she be given tea with the servants, or in the drawing room?

But in the towns Flora Thompson's "bettermost people" were far more obtrusive. When the narrator, Laura, goes to work in the village of Candleford Green, she realizes this for herself.

"The population of Candleford Green was more varied. It had a clergyman of its own and doctor and independent gentlewomen who lived in superior cottages with stabling attached, and artisans and labourers who lived in smaller and poorer ones, though none so small and poor as those of the hamlet. Then there were shopkeepers and the schoolmaster and a master builder and the villa people who lived on the new building estate outside the village."

All these, excluding the artisans and the labourers, might be called members of the middle class, though this is not what they would have called themselves. The doctor and the clergyman would have called themselves "gentlemen" and neither they nor the independent gentlewomen would have dreamed of mingling socially with those who made their money from trade, such as the Candleford Green master builder – who well might be considerably wealthier than themselves.

As Candleford Green society was more complex than the hamlet where Laura had been brought up, so was the society of a country town or a city more complex than Candleford Green. There you might encounter wealthy manufacturers who lived in princely style, heads of great business houses like Mr. Dombey who stalks majestically through the pages of Dickens' *Dombey and Son*, never doubting for one moment that he is a prince of the land.

In the cities might be encountered a section of the middle class whom neither Matthew Arnold nor Laura named: the educated élite from whom Arnold himself sprang, who were, as the century progressed and inherited social rank counted for less and less, to provide the headmasters, the bishops, the university teachers, the senior civil servants and the politicians of late Victorian England. But all these, widely different in their lives, their interests, their incomes and their social habits though they were – the Arnolds, Mr. Dombey, the little gentlewomen in Mrs. Gaskell's novel *Cranford* who struggled to keep up appearances on a hundred pounds a year, the tradesmen from whom they bought their goods, and Mr. Pooter with his genteel villa "The Laurels, Brickfield Terrace, Holloway, a nice six-roomed residence, not counting basement, with a front breakfast-parlour" all these are middle class. Even if they are divided again, into upper and lower middle class, the divisions within these divisions are enormous, and the antagonism that one section might feel for another might be very strong. The Victorian novel deals in much detail with the differences that separate one stratum from another – differences in speech, dress, times of eating; whether one went to Church or Chapel, educated one's daughters at home or at a local school, addressed one's father as "Father", or "Papa" or "Pa".

In the early days, before the middle class had held such a huge variety of elements, the opposition in the main had been between landowners and manufacturers, who stood in general for two different sets of interests. "I find that nothing seems to be considered so decided a stigma, as to brand a man as a mill-owner," wrote Cobden to his brother after there had been bitter exchanges in the House of Commons over the Corn Laws, and the whole class of northern manufacturers had been denounced by the country gentlemen as vicious exploiters of human misery. Long after the political issues had died down there continued to be suspicion and dislike among the aristocracy and gentry for those who had acquired their money through manufacture or trade. There was a Lady Suffield in the mid-19th century who became very angry if asked to meet anyone she considered socially inferior. On one occasion, seeing at a party someone who had begun life as a miller, she remarked loudly, "I can scarcely see across the room owing to all this flour dust."

George Eliot in *Middlemarch*, a study of provincial society in 1830–32, describes how remote the lives of the landowning gentry were from the manufacturers and tradesmen in the neighbouring town. "The country gentry of old time lived in a rarified social air; dotted apart on their stations up the mountain they looked down with imperfect discrimination on the belts of thicker life below." A knot of these gentry gathers in the library window of Lowick manor to look down at the funeral in the churchyard below of a Middlemarch worthy. They are serious, well-meaning people, but they treat it as though it were a raree show. The wife of the clergyman officiating at the funeral admits that she has come because she wants to see "collections of strange animals such as there would be at this funeral." "'Lovegood tells me the old fellow has left a good deal of money as well as land,'" remarks one of the watchers. "'Think of that now! when so many younger sons can't dine at their own expense,'" responds the clergyman's wife, apparently feeling that all money should be in the hands of the gentry. Then she scrutinizes the mourners as they leave the church, trying to identify them and to account for their presence.

"'Ah! now they are coming out of church,' Mrs. Cadwallader exclaimed. 'Dear me, what a wonderfully mixed set! Mr. Lydgate as doctor, I suppose. But that is really a good-looking woman, and the fair young man must be her son. Who are they, Sir James, do you know?'

'I see Vincy, the Mayor of Middlemarch; they are probably his wife and son,' said Sir James, looking interrogatively at Mr. Brooke, who nodded, and said—

'Yes, a very decent family – a very good fellow is Vincy; a credit to the manufacturing interest . . .'

'A coursing fellow, though,' said Sir James, with a fox-hunter's disgust.

'And one of those who suck the life out of the wretched handloom weavers in Tipton and Freshitt. That is how his family look so fair and sleek,' said Mrs. Cadwallader."

Here we have all the prejudice of the old ways for the new, the dislike of the urban civilization by the landed gentry, who argue that the mill-owners are driving the handloom workers out of business.

In reverse, the Middlemarch worthies feel awed reverence for the gentry. Even Rosamond Lydgate, the Middlemarch doctor's wife, educated as she has been at one of the best local schools (where they taught her every ladylike accomplishment from music to how to descend gracefully from a carriage), dressed in the height of fashion and conscious of her beauty, feels deep emotion at an unexpected visit from Dorothea Casaubon. "To Rosamund she was one of those county divinities not mixing with Middlemarch mortality, whose slightest marks of manner or appearance were worthy of her study."

The prejudice felt by the old-established gentry for "trade" lingered on long after the original political differences had died down. It was held, particularly by ladies, that those who had made their money from "trade" did not know how to behave, were vulgar and over-dressed. Mrs. Ewing in *Lob Lie-by-the-Fire*, voiced the prejudices of her sex and class when she described the attitude of two impoverished gentlewomen towards the daughter of a manufacturer who dressed herself in the finest quality clothes, but spoilt the effect by not being able to bear herself with dignity.

"'And how should she know how to walk?' said Miss Betty. 'Her mother can't have taught her, poor body! that ran through the streets of Leith, with a creel on her back, as a lassie; and got out of her coach (lined with satin, do you mind, sister Kitty?) to her dying day, with a bounce, all in a heap, her dress caught, and her stockings exposed (among ourselves, ladies!) like some good wife that's afraid to be late for the market. Aye, aye! Malcolm Midden – good man! – made a fine pocket of silver in a dirty trade, but his women'll jerk, and toss, and bounce, and fuss, and fluster for a generation or two yet, for all the silks and satins he can buy 'em.'"

Even Mr. Pooter, the city clerk with his dingy little Holloway villa, feels a genteel superiority to tradesmen – although they could (as one of them is discourteous enough to inform Mr. Pooter) "buy up 'things' like you by the dozen!" In this Mr. Pooter, as in many other matters, reflects the attitude of a bygone age. *The Diary of a Nobody*, published in 1894, is a study of late-Victorian gentility, and the Pooters and others of their kind are shown clinging to outmoded notions about the difference between the man who works in a black coat and white collar at a desk and the man who handles money behind a shop counter.

Mr. Pooter's genteel villa in Holloway.

Mr. Pooter hangs up a
plaster-of-Paris stag's head
to give his hall "style".

Mr. Pooter's fellow clerks scoff at his new trousers.
Drawings by Weedon Grossmith from *The Diary of a Nobody*.

There is a great moment in Mr. Pooter's life when he receives an invitation to a reception given by the Lord Mayor. It is a big red-letter day, as he himself describes it, and the preparations for the reception occupy the Pooter household for days. But to his horrified amazement there he meets "Farmerson, our ironmonger."

"He said, in the most familiar way: 'This is better than Brickfield Terrace, eh?' I simply looked at him, and said coolly: 'I never expected to see you here.' He said, with a loud, coarse laugh: 'I like that – if *you*, why not *me*?' I replied: 'Certainly.' I wish I could have thought of something better to say. He said: 'Can I get your good lady anything?' Carrie said: 'No, I thank you,' for which I was pleased. I said, by way of reproof to him: 'You never sent to-day to paint the bath, as I requested,' Farmerson said: 'Pardon me, Mr. Pooter, no shop when we're in company, please.'

Before I could think of a reply, one of the sheriffs, in full Court costume, slapped Farmerson on the back and hailed him as an old friend, and asked him to dine with him at his lodge. I was astonished. For full five minutes they stood roaring with laughter, and digging each other in the ribs. They kept telling each other they didn't look a day older. They began embracing each other and drinking champagne.

To think that a man who mends our scraper should know any member of our aristocracy!"

Here George Grossmith demonstrates the naivety of Mr. Pooter. A sheriff of the City of London would be no aristocrat, but a wealthy and successful businessman whose origins might have been the same as the ironmonger's.

But whatever the Mr. Pooters and the Victorian gentlewomen might think, there was as much movement within the middle class as there always had been throughout the English class system, a continual struggling of the abler members towards the top. This might take more time than it would in one of the newer countries, but in two or three generations the descendants of a dogged and determined artisan might find themselves governing England.

The professional men who became the new leaders of England when the old aristocratic privileges disappeared were members of the middle class. A young man at the beginning of the 19th century might do well in trade or industry. The evangelical religion that was so marked a feature of those years might fire his children not only with religious zeal but with a desire to improve themselves, and inspire them to seek a good education for their own children. The grandchildren of this successful tradesman, then, educated at a public school and university, would be raised considerably above the social level of their grandfather. They would be able to mingle on easy terms with the aristocratic and landed families, and they would find – for by now we are in the later decades of the 19th century – that high positions in the Army, the Civil Service and the Church, hitherto reserved for those with aristocratic influence, were open to them if they had the ability. New professions too were coming into existence. Medicine was attracting men of ability and education, there was revived life in the universities and schools, and posts as university teachers and headmasters were eagerly sought. It was not the aristocracy who dominated the late Victorian scene, but families such as the Trevelyans, the Macaulays, the Huxleys, the Stephens and the Arnolds, who had risen from origins such as have been described, who had intermarried and formed enormous clans, and had worked their way to great heights in academic life, in the professions, and in the literary world.

At the beginning of Victoria's reign the professions hardly existed in England. There was the Church, law, the army; for all these money and influence of the sort that only the aristocracy could provide were needed. There was too the Civil Service, but at that time it was so small and so much the preserve of the aristocracy that the Liberal John Bright, who was one of the leaders of the manufacturing class in their opposition to the land-owning class, described it as outdoor relief for the aristocracy, a stinging remark with its implication that the aristocracy were as unemployable on their own merits as an unskilled pauper, and as in any case outdoor relief for paupers had been abandoned in 1834 there was further insult in suggesting that arrangements involving the aristocracy were of course hopelessly behind the times.

There was also India, which during the 18th century had provided fat rewards for those who could survive its climate. Alexis de Tocqueville summed up the situation in 1835 as he had found it during his visit to England.

"Q What are the openings for the younger branches of the aristocracy?
 A *Firstly*, the Established Church; generally the great landowners have rights of nomination to some well-endowed livings.

Secondly, the Bar [i.e. the legal profession]; one must start by being quite rich to qualify. The rich landowner makes this initial expendi-ture for his son, and by this means the son finds himself in an élite body, where competition is necessarily limited as great means are required to enter into it.

Thirdly, the army; commissions are bought; a soldier almost never becomes an officer.

Fourthly, the great resort is India. India offers quite a large number of positions at enormous salaries, £10,000[1] for example; the aristocracy pushes its younger sons in that direction. It is an inex-haustible resource for it, all the more because the climate is so deadly that the odds are three to one that an Englishman will die there; but if he does not die, he is *sure* of getting rich."

De Tocqueville does not mention the Civil Service, but otherwise he gives a fair picture of things as they were at the beginning of Queen Victoria's reign.

Reforms were slow in coming, but by the 1870's the purchase system in the Army was abolished, staff colleges were set up to train officers, a com-petitive system for entry into the Civil Service was introduced, and the scope for the professional man seeking a career was enormously widened.

1 A colossal sum at a time when a middle class man could live comfortably on £100 a year, and one that it would take a huge establishment or much gambling to spend.

For the most part such men had been educated at the public schools which during this late Victorian period were in their golden age, fired with the spirit that Thomas Arnold[1] had infused into Rugby fifty years before.

When Arnold had become headmaster of Rugby in 1827 the great English public schools – Eton, Harrow, Winchester and the others – were at a low ebb. Parents who could well have afforded to send their sons there often avoided them, dismayed by the accounts of the squalor, cruelty and unruliness.

We can get some idea of the disorder that prevailed from two stories by Maria Edgeworth[2] which touch on school life in the pre-Arnold era. In *The Barring Out* she describes a school mutiny, where boys dissatisfied with their headmaster barricade themselves into a classroom and prepare to stay there until he capitulates. In *The Good Aunt* there is an account of Westminster at the beginning of the century – a place where the boys are completely unsupervised, and provided they show up the prescribed Latin and Greek exercises their behaviour is not investigated. The villain of the piece, young Augustus Holloway, is consumed with ambition to drive a coach and four. The master in whose house he lodges is an indolent man, and as long as he is left in peace to practise his flute he does not care in the least that young Augustus half murders the younger boys, spends most of his time conversing with stablemen, runs a lottery in the school, and creeps off the premises at night "whilst his tutor was yet in the middle of a long concerto" in order to drive a stage coach (which he does so recklessly, that he overturns it).

This was the state of things that Arnold found at Rugby. He was there for only fifteen years until he died in 1842, but he influenced profoundly the whole course of English public school education. He was determined that Rugby should turn out "Christian gentlemen", responsible, conscientious, able to lead and to set a good example.

The English public school system had always assumed that boys were to be left for a large portion of their time to form an independent society of their own, in which the influence that they exercise over each other is far greater than can possibly be exercised by the masters. Great evils can

1 Thomas Arnold (1795–1842). One of the great Victorian headmasters who had a profound influence on the course of English public school education.

2 Maria Edgeworth (1767–1849). Novelist, who also wrote a number of excellent children's stories.

result from such a system, and these Arnold sought to eliminate, not by stern disciplinary methods, but by appeals to the boys themselves. His sermons in the Rugby school chapel played a vital part in forming the new spirit of conscientious, earnest endeavour that he infused into the school and that spread to the other English public schools – both the ancient foundations, that had been like savage bear-pits a few years before, and the new schools that were founded during Victoria's reign. He did not aim to produce intellectual prodigies, but boys who were capable of using the freedom and independence of school life as a preparation for life in the world outside. "It is not necessary that this should be a school for three hundred, or even one hundred, boys, but it is necessary that it should be a school of Christian gentlemen." Acting on this, he made a practice of treating the boys as gentlemen and reasonable beings, of making them respect themselves by the respect he showed to them; of showing that he appealed and trusted to their own common sense and conscience.

Tom Brown's Schooldays was published in 1857, fifteen years after Arnold's death, and did a great deal to awaken interest in Arnold's methods. The author, Thomas Hughes, had been at Rugby in Arnold's time, and the book shows how the new conscientious spirit was beginning

TOM BROWN DEFENDS ARTHUR AGAINST THE
DORMITORY BULLIES
Illustration from the 1869 edition of *Tom Brown's Schooldays.*

to take effect on the old lawless society. Tom Brown himself belongs by nature to the lawless set. He is a slapdash, cheerful, unthinking boy who, unchecked, would have adapted himself quite easily to the old bear-pit ways. He would have stumbled through the desired amount of Greek and Latin, preparing it with the help of a "crib", he would have fought, drunk at the local beer-house, poached in the neighbouring fields and woods, punched the heads of the smaller boys and, while meaning no harm, would have left a trail of havoc behind him.

But with the spirit of "the Doctor" dominating the school, Tom's conscience is stirred. He undertakes to look after and protect a younger, weaker boy, he gives up many of his wilder pursuits, he agrees to abandon the use of a crib in preparing his lessons. He will never be anything of a scholar, perhaps he will never attain the heights of the Sixth form, the élite of Rugby whom Arnold taught himself and who were closest to him, but he will carry away with him a code of behaviour which will mark him out through his whole life as a product of the English public school system as reformed by Arnold.

"'I want to be A1 at cricket and football, and all the other games, and to make my hands keep my head against any fellow, lout or gentleman. I want to get into the sixth before I leave, and to please the Doctor; and I want to carry away just as much Latin and Greek as will take me through Oxford respectably ... [and] I want to leave behind me,' said Tom speaking low and looking much moved, 'the name of a fellow who never bullied a little boy or turned his back on a big one.'"

Matthew Arnold's poem *Rugby Chapel* is one of the best expressions of the feeling that Dr. Arnold's pupils had for him. It opens with an evocative description of the school itself, which expresses the emotion that many feel when they revisit their schools.

> "Coldly, sadly descends
> The autumn evening. The field
> Strewn with its dank yellow drifts
> Of wither'd leaves, and the elms,
> Fade into dimness apace,
> Silent; – hardly a shout
> From a few boys late at their play!
> The lights come out in the street,

In the school-room windows; – but cold,
Solemn, unlighted, austere,
Through the gathering darkness, arise
The chapel-walls, in whose bound
Thou, my father! art laid.

. . . . .

Yes, in some far-shining sphere,
Conscious or not of the past,
Still thou performest the word
Of the Spirit in whom thou dost live –
Prompt, unwearied, as here!
Still thou upraisest with zeal
The humble good from the ground,
Sternly repressest the bad!
Still, like a trumpet, dost rouse
Those who with half-open eyes
Tread the border-land dim
'Twixt vice and virtue, reviv'st,
Succourest! – this was thy work,
This was thy life upon earth."

The Arnold ethos affected the school stories of the mid-Victorian era. After *Tom Brown's School-days* the most famous of those that touch on the temptations of public school life, the moral victories and defeats, is Dean Farrar's *Eric, or Little by Little* (1858). Eric, unlike Tom Brown, is defeated by what he meets at school, so hopelessly corrupted by the evil he encounters for the first time in his life that Dean Farrar feels his sins can only be expiated by death. Some would see in this a condemnation of the public school system, but this is far from Farrar's intention. "The true preparation for life, the true basis of a manly character, is not to have been ignorant of evil, but to have known it and avoided it; not to have been sheltered from tempta-tion, but to have passed through it and overcome it by God's help."

Much was to be written of godliness and manliness in reference to the education of Victorian boys. But manliness as understood by the early and mid-Victorians did not include reserve and a stiff upper lip. This was a much later development. Both in reality and in fiction, there were frequent, unashamed displays of emotion in boys' schools. Boys wept and flung their

SCHOOLBOY FRIENDSHIP
An illustration from the 1869 edition of *Tom Brown's Schooldays*.

arms round each other as they protested eternal friendship; they threw
themselves on the ground and clasped their masters' knees as they expressed
their penitence, the schoolboys at Wellington wept as they heard their
headmaster's last sermon. Master and pupil would kneel together to pray
for guidance, a headmaster and his staff sometimes wept during staff meetings if there was a difference of opinion, friendships between boys and
between master and pupil were of an intensity that would now be considered dangerous. This must be borne in mind by the modern reader of
Tom Brown and *Eric*. The scenes where the dying Arthur persuades Tom
to give up the use of cribs in preparing his Latin; or where Eric, on his knees,
"his blue eyes drowned with tears," implores the headmaster to show
leniency towards his friend, are not extravagant inventions of the writers
concerned, but were perfectly possible in the emotional climate of the
mid-19th century.

Other public schools followed Rugby's lead. To prepare boys for
responsible service became their ideal, and this new seriousness attracted
parents who before would have sent their boys to the local grammar school

or to a private tutor (as Tom Tulliver[1] was sent to board with a clergyman). Sons of landed gentry mingled at school with the sons of the new class that had made its money from manufacture or trade and through this the great social divide between the landlords and the business men was bridged, and the new middle class began to emerge, the class that was to fill the professions, govern England's empire overseas, and eventually to wrest the government of England itself from the aristocrats.

A girl's education was a very different matter, and it was not until much later in the century that the influence of Miss Buss and Miss Beale (the founders respectively of the North London Collegiate School and Cheltenham Ladies College) resulted in the founding of High Schools where girls from a variety of different backgrounds could be given a solid background of learning.

The Victorian girl of good family was usually educated at home. She might be taught by her mother, or by a resident governess, or by an older member of the family, and it says much for the discipline and orderly life of a Victorian household that girls did often manage to achieve a fair degree of learning under such circumstances. Some of them, indeed, did more than that, and there are touching accounts of girls wrestling with foreign languages, translating Dante and Schiller, poring over Greek and Latin grammars; trying to wrest from books alone the school or university education that was denied to them.

Charlotte Yonge's[2] domestic novels are full of girls ardently pursuing learning. Miss Yonge, who had been taught first by her mother and then by her father at home, insisted that this was the best possible education, and looked with suspicion and disfavour at the new High Schools that by the last years of the century, when she was an old woman, were springing into being, and attracting girls from the sort of family that would, when she was young, have kept their daughters cloistered at home. The heroines of her novels are bookish and cultured, but Miss Yonge always insists that learning must come second to their womanly duties in the house. Ethel May, for instance, in *The Daisy Chain*, a gawky, awkward bluestocking, has to learn to put aside the Latin grammar that she delights

1 In George Eliot's *The Mill on the Floss*.
2 Charlotte Mary Yonge (1823–1901). Author of one hundred and sixty books, including historical tales and domestic chronicles. Influenced by John Keble whose religious views she echoed in her fiction.

in, and devote herself to more womanly pursuits when these are required
of her. Meta Rivers, in the same book, knows that she must amuse her elder
brother before she can attend to her own studies. Only when she has sung
him and her father to sleep in the drawing room in the evenings does she
feel free to pick up the book she longs to study – Thirlwall's *Greece*.

Out-of-date shibboleths and tabus there are in Charlotte Yonge's
novels, but what shines through them is an impressive "goodness" and
a feeling for spiritual values. The characters in her books are families such
as she knew herself – the Moberlys, for instance, children of the headmaster of Winchester who later became Bishop of Salisbury – large, united,
affectionate families, country-dwelling, immersed in their parish affairs,
bookish, full of zest for learning. She has left a verbatim record of the
animated chatter of her cousins one evening which corresponds exactly to
the dialogue of one of her imaginary families. Charlotte Yonge mirrors
the domestic life of the mid-Victorian leisured classes at its best, and shows
us a quiet happiness and steadiness of purpose.

The girl ardently pursuing learning by herself was no myth. We have
an actual example in Emily Shore who died in 1839 of consumption at
the age of nineteen. Her journal contains a record of her plans for her studies.
"I cannot bear the idea of living, even in sickness," she wrote when she was
seventeen and already knew that she was gravely ill, "without systematically
acquiring knowledge. So I shall devote myself at present to making myself
mistress of history, chronology, and geography; the study of languages,
mathematics, arithmetic, and the science of mechanics, etc., I must leave
till I am quite restored to health." Remorselessly she spurs herself onwards;
fearing that her life will be cut short, she dreads lest a single moment should
be wasted. While she dresses she repeats a chapter from the Bible; in the
evening while she undresses she goes over in her mind a chart of genealogy.
While she curls her hair she learns from the New Testament. Charts and
tables are pinned to her walls so that she can absorb knowledge whenever
she raises her eyes.

Emily Shore and Charlotte Yonge's heroines were of course gifted girls
who in these days would receive a university education. The average girl
was not capable of such devotion to learning nor of such self-discipline.
For the ordinary run of middle class girls there was the resident governess,
or, less frequently, a small boarding school of some thirty pupils who would
be drilled in accomplishments and in an array of facts which would be

taught parrot-wise. There are many accounts of such establishments in Victorian fiction, from Miss Pinkerton's Academy in *Vanity Fair* to Miss Twinkleton's Seminary in *Edwin Drood*.

One of the most convincing accounts of this sort of education comes in Mrs. Ewing's *Six to Sixteen*.[1] Bush House is not grossly ill-managed nor inhumane. It is just run without any sort of imagination. The school is owned by two gentlewomen who employ a French governess to do the hard work, and a collection of visiting masters to teach such matters as arithmetic and drawing. The girls are over-worked, ill-fed, and irked by the nagging

Punch JOKES AT MIDDLE CLASS SNOBBERY
Miss Prunes. "Ah Doctor, these High Schools are sadly mixed! But, under *my* care, I can assure you that your little ward will associate with daughters of *gentlemen* only!"
The Doctor. "That, Madam, is to be select indeed, since I believe Pallas Athene alone fulfilled such a condition."
Many Victorians would have shared Miss Prunes' distrust of High Schools, for the same reason. Du Maurier drawing, *Punch,* 1892.

1 G. M. Young classes *Six to Sixteen* with Ruskin's *Praeterita*, Mrs. Hughes's *A London Child of the Seventies*, the anonymous *Book with Seven Seals*, and *David Copperfield*, as the books which, taken together, give the truest idea of family life, its standards and morals, in the Victorian age.

of those in authority. Their only exercise is to file through the streets escorted by the French governess. They must talk in French during their recreation; only on Sundays is English permitted. Their health suffers from this régime, their temper from the over-zealous supervision – "that excess of meddle-some discipline which seems to be *de rigeur* in girls' schools."

The ethos of the English public school tradition as formulated by Arnold – the training of the pupil in self-discipline and responsibility, preparing him to govern others as well as himself – never penetrated to the Victorian girls' school. The middle class Victorians liked to think that their boys had been exposed to evil and had rejected it, but insisted that their girls should be constantly supervised and chaperoned and protected from the faintest breath of temptation. "'Oh! lucky baby, to have so many years to come before you are plagued with troublesome propriety!'" whispers Margaret May in *The Daisy Chain* to her infant sister when it is considered that it would be improper for her to go on a walk with her brothers and sisters and the governess because a young male friend of the family proposes to accompany them.

Schools for the gentleman's daughter were not the usual practice, more common was the resident governess, an untrained gentlewoman, who might offer loving devotion to her charges but rarely had any qualifications whatever for teaching them, beyond what she had absorbed herself at school. Governesses abound in Victorian fiction. It was the only refuge of the middle-class female if the family fortunes collapsed around her and left no money for her support. The most famous of the Victorian governesses are undoubtedly Charlotte, Emily, and Anne Brontë, of whom Charlotte and Anne have left gloomy accounts of their experiences in *Jane Eyre* and *Agnes Grey*. They describe with savage intensity the insolence with which they were treated, the inordinate amount of work that was expected of them, the indiscipline of their pampered little charges, and above all, the humiliations to which they were exposed ("Love the *governess*, my dear!" said one mother in the presence of the children, when a little boy had told Charlotte Brontë that he loved her.) Against this, it must be remembered that any persons less suited to their task than the Brontës can hardly be imagined. Sad, low-spirited, morbidly sensitive, with no experience of childish high spirits, they must have been depressing companions. Mrs. Gaskell in her *Life of Charlotte Brontë*, admits their unsuitability.

"Teaching seemed to [Charlotte] at that time, as it does to most women at all times, the only way of earning an independent livelihood. But neither she nor her sisters were naturally fond of children. The hieroglyphics of childhood were an unknown language to them, for they had never been much with those younger than themselves. I am inclined to think, too, that they had not the happy knack of imparting information."

So far we have hardly touched on the Philistine element of the Victorian middle class. Matthew Arnold called them Philistines because, he said, they were stiff-necked and inflexible, "the enemy of the children of light," lured off from light by worldly splendour, security, power and pleasure. "The graver self of one kind of Philistine likes fanaticism, business, and money-making; his more relaxed self, comfort and tea-meetings," wrote Arnold, referring to prosperous chapel-goers who practised a fanatical type of Protestantism and nourished a violent hatred for Roman Catholicism and the High Church party of the Church of England. Their ambitions, he said, could best be summarized by the sentence that the mother of Sir Daniel Gooch, the railway magnate, repeated to her son every morning when he was a boy going to work: "Ever remember, my dear Dan, that you should look forward to being some day manager of that concern!" And they smugly sat, according to Arnold, contemplating the cities they had built, the railroads they had made, the manufactures they had produced, and "the cargoes which freight the ships of the largest mercantile navy the world has ever seen."

Mr. Dombey is an arch-Philistine, with no emotion to spare except for his firm of Dombey and Son; with no affection to give his daughter since she cannot perpetuate his name in the firm, with all his gratification and all his disappointments drawn solely from the fortunes of Dombey and Son.

On a lower level the congregation of Salem Chapel in Mrs. Oliphant's novel of that name are Philistines. Here Mrs. Oliphant[1] shows a collection of people not only with a fondness for comfortable living and a sharp eye for business, but with the religious intolerance that Arnold had mentioned. To this congregation of "greengrocers, dealers in cheese and bacon, milkmen, with some dressmakers of inferior pretensions, and teachers

1 Margaret Oliphant, née Wilson (1828–97). Voluminous writer of novels, of which her *Chronicles of Carlingford* are the best known. *Salem Chapel* is a novel in this series.

of day-schools of similar humble character" comes a young minister with lofty ideals, and ideas about how dormant minds will awake under his influence. He is dismayed to find how much of his duty consists of eating his way through a large six o'clock tea with the dealer in cheese and bacon or the dairyman ("'All our own folks, sir, and a comfortable evening; and prayers, if you'll *be* so good, at the end'"). The chapel deacon refers to the numbers of the congregation as though he were dealing in pounds of butter: "'Three more pews applied for this week – fifteen sittings in all,' said Mr. Tozer; 'that's what I call satisfactory, that is. We mustn't let the steam go down – not on no account. You keep well at them of Sundays, Mr. Vincent, and trust to the managers, sir, to keep 'em up to their dooty.'" If the minister can keep the steam up, then the congregation will be able to add £50 to his salary next year, and the deacon suggests that a course of sermons attacking bishops and the Established Church might be a promising line to pursue. "A life of jealousy of the Establishment, disputes, tea-meetings, openings of chapels, sermons," was how Matthew Arnold described this aspect of his middle-class Philistines.

The Victorian Philistines also dealt in education as though it were a commodity to be measured in terms of money and respectability. George Eliot in her studies of provincial society: *Middlemarch* and *The Mill on the Floss,* touches on this. Mr. Vincy, the prosperous Middlemarch manu-facturer, sends his son to the university in the expectation that he will then go into the Church and become a gentleman, and is very aggrieved when Fred is disinclined to do so; he feels that the money has been thrown away on the boy. Mr. Tulliver in *The Mill on the Floss* also sees education as some-thing that a prudent man buys for his son as an insurance for the boy's future. "'Now what I want is to send him to a school where they'll make him a bit nimble with his tongue and his pen, and make a smart chap of him. I want my son to be even wi' those fellows as have got the start o' me with having better schooling.'" £150 a year is a little steep for such a com-modity, £100 is a fair price – Mr. Tulliver treats the matter as though he were bargaining for corn at the local corn exchange.

The Victorian middle class boy, unless he went to a public school, was ill-served when it came to education. The grammar schools where, in the old days, the squire's son and the farmer's bright son might have sat side by side and prepared their Latin, had decayed. The Victorian squire sent his son to a public school, the tradesman and the farmer now clamoured

AT THE GREAT EXHIBITION, 1851

Middle class visitors inspect household furnishings. (Dickinson's *Comprehensive Pictures of the Great Exhibition*.)

(c) Radio Times Hulton Picture Library.

for a "commercial education" for their boys, something that the ancient grammar schools, limited by the terms of those that had endowed them to the teaching of the classics, were unable to provide.

The view of the tradesmen was much the same as Mr. Tulliver's view on the subject of Tom's education: "'I want him to know figures, and write like print, and see into things quick, and know what folks mean, and how to wrap things up in words as aren't actionable.'" Tom, in the end, is sent to a clergyman's house, where, with one other pupil, he does in fact learn a certain amount of Latin and Euclid. Many clergymen took in pupils at this time. Dr. Arnold himself, before he went to Rugby, had a private establishment at Laleham, near Staines, where he prepared seven or eight boys for the university. This sort of education was, however, usually an alternative to a public school; the tradesmen preferred to send their sons to a commercial academy, where they would be taught to write a good copperplate hand and cast up long lines of figures. H. G. Wells[1] in *Kipps* (1905) drew on memories of his own private school in the late 1870's when he described "Cavendish Academy".

"It was called an Academy for Young Gentlemen, and many of the young gentlemen had parents in 'India' and other unverifiable places. Others were the sons of credulous widows, anxious, as Kipps' mother had been, to get something a little 'superior' to a board school education as cheaply as possible, and others, again, were sent to demonstrate the dignity of their parents and guardians...

Its 'principal' was a lean, long creature of indifferent digestion and temper, who proclaimed himself on a gilt lettered board in his front area, George Garden Woodrow, F.S.Sc., letters indicating that he had paid certain guineas for a bogus diploma. A bleak, whitewashed outhouse constituted his schoolroom, and the scholastic quality of its carved and worn desks and forms were enhanced by a slippery blackboard and two large, yellow, out-of-date maps – one of Africa and the other of Wiltshire – that he had picked up cheap at a sale. There were other maps and globes in his study, where he interviewed inquiring parents, but these his pupils never saw. And in a glass cupboard in the passage were several shillings-worth of test-tubes and chemicals, a tripod, a glass retort, and a damaged Bunsen burner, manifesting that the 'scientific laboratory' mentioned in the prospectus was no idle boast."

Perhaps the spirit of schools such as these, and the parents to serve whose demands the schools existed, is best conveyed in a book written many decades later. In George Orwell's[2] *A Clergyman's Daughter* (1935) the heroine goes to teach in a miserable private school for girls. Appalled by the curriculum, which consists largely of copying in copperplate writing, she initiates more imaginative lessons. But at the end of her first fortnight a parent writes to her:

---

1 Herbert George Wells (1866–1946). First successful English author of science fiction; also wrote novels of middle class life such as *Kipps* and *The History of Mr. Polly*.
2 George Orwell, pseudonym of Eric Blair (1903–50). Author of political satires expressing disillusionment with Communism, as well as novels which mirror with deep pessimism some of the episodes in his own career.

"Dear Miss. Would you please give Mabel a bit more *arithmetic*. I feel that what your giving her is not practacle enough. All these maps and that. She wants practacle work, not all this fancy stuff. So more *arithmetic*, please. And remain,

Yours Faithfully,

GEO. BRIGGS.

P.S. Mabel says your talking of starting her on something called decimals. I don't want her taught decimals, I want her taught *arithmetic*."

Another parent writes complaining that her child is being given Shakes-peare to read. "For her own part she had never so much as been to the pictures in her life, let alone to a stage-play, and she felt that even in *reading* stage-plays there was a very grave danger,' etc., etc. She gave way, however, on being informed that Mr. Shakespeare was dead."

Here, of course, Orwell exaggerates wildly, but in spite of this and in spite of the fact that it was written in 1935 it does convey the materialism and the Puritanism that was so marked a feature of Victorian lower middle class life, and which lingered on far into the 20th century.

Victorian respectability was in marked contrast to the coarseness of the earlier aristocrat-dominated age. "I have been told," wrote G. W. E. Russell, reflecting on the differences between Victorian and Georgian manners, "by one who heard it from an eye-witness, that a great Whig duchess . . . turning to the footman who was waiting on her at dinner, exclaimed, 'I wish to G— that you wouldn't keep rubbing your great greasy belly against the back of my chair.'" This is far removed indeed from the behaviour of polite Victorian society where it was grossly improper to mention such words as "stomach".

As the influence of the evangelical movement spread in the early decades of the 19th century, a new seriousness and conscientiousness took posses-sion of the nation, and the grosser kinds of cruelty, extravagance and profligacy were driven underground. The evangelicals, said G. M. Young, established a certain level of behaviour for all who wished to stand well with their fellows. "In moralizing society they had made social dis-approval a force which the boldest sinner might fear."

Respectability became a fetish, and so entangled with religious observ-ance that few could say where genuine piety ended and a wish to stand well in the eyes of one's fellows began. Respectability was the outstanding

VICTORIAN RESPECTABILITY

"But why don't you send for Dr. Masher, Aunt Jane? He's the cleverest doctor
in the whole country!"

"Oh, my dear, I couldn't! He *dresses* so irreligiously!"

Drawing from *Punch,* 1892.

characteristic of Matthew Arnold's Philistines, and respectability included
comfortable living and a comfortable sufficiency of material possessions
as well as attendance at church or chapel, and a proper observance of
Sunday. George Eliot conveys all this in her description of Mrs. Tulliver's
sisters:

"The religion of the Dodsons consisted of revering whatever was customary
and respectable: it was necessary to be baptised, else one could not be buried
in the churchyard, and to take the sacrament before death as a security
against more simply understood perils; but it was of equal necessity to

have the proper pall-bearers and well-cured hams at one's funerals, and
to leave an unimpeachable will."

George Eliot is here writing of an early 19th century country society, but
in essence this is the spirit of Matthew Arnold's Philistines: the conviction
that respectability is what matters most in life, and that to be respectable
one must live comfortably, and pay due attention to the religious forms
and social conventions around one, without, however, distinguishing
one from the other.

The Dodson sisters set much store by the possession of cupboards full of
china and glass (which they are far too prudent to use), and in the right
bonnet for church. There is a scene in *The Mill on the Floss* where Mrs.
Pullet in the presence of her sister, her nephew, and her niece displays her
new bonnet. First she extracts a key from among layers of linen in a ward-
robe. This opens the door of a darkened room where the furniture is
shrouded. Here, in a locked cupboard, hidden in tissue paper, reposes
The Bonnet, which she unveils with the air of one exhibiting a sacred relic
to supremely privileged pilgrims. "Mrs. Pullet screwed up her mouth and
shook her head, and then whispered, 'Pullet pays for it; he said I was to
have the best bonnet at Garum Church, let the next best be whose it would.'"

There may have been genuine reasons why so many of the evangelical
middle class families of the early Victorian years thought it proper to abstain
from fashionable forms of recreation, such as dancing, card-playing and
the theatre, and kept Sunday with as much rigour as if it were the Jewish
Sabbath, but respectability was mixed in with the piety. It was respectable
to attend church twice on Sundays, to hold family prayers for the whole
household in the mornings, and to say grace before meals. Emma Jane
Worboise, who wrote evangelical tales for the family circle, in *Heart's
Ease in the Family* (1874) describes with some indignation how a thoroughly
worldly family, ambitious that its daughters should be well brought up,
feels that Sunday should be kept in the schoolroom:

"Before breakfast we must say the collect and six verses of a psalm out of
the French Prayer-book, which is by no means a blessing. After breakfast
we read Josephus aloud to Miss Shepherd . . . then we go to church and take
notes of the sermon; which, after dinner, we condense and put into rational
form. Then we attend church again sometimes; if we stay at home we say

the Church Catechism, and learn pieces of sacred poetry till tea-time; after tea, we repeat a chapter in the Bible, which we have 'got up' during the week, and also the Gospel for the day; and we read Blair's or somebody's sermons till nearly eight o'clock, and then we go into the drawing-room and play sacred music till nine, when supper is ready in the schoolroom, and as soon as that is over we go to bed."

Miss Worboise attacks here the outward observance of Sunday by those to whom it was only a social convention. Sabbatarianism was a great feature of Victorian middle class respectability, the prohibitions were endless, and one can best get an idea of these from some of the children's literature of the period. Most of the writers who dwelt on the proper observation of the Sabbath concentrated on the negative aspects – what one might not do on a Sunday – and rarely contrived to give any purpose for all these rulings.

Perhaps the sternest of all the books on this subject is *The Children's Tabernacle* (1871) by A.L.O.E.,[1] initials which stood for A Lady of England. Here a family of children is building a model of the Jewish Tabernacle to display to a Ragged School. Dora, carried away by enthusiasm, ventures to stitch the curtains on a Sunday. She argues with herself:

"There are some things which even mamma says are quite lawful to be done on Sundays, such as charitable works. Mamma herself dressed the cook's scalded arm on a Sunday, and put a stitch or two to keep the bandages firm. *That* was surely sewing on a Sunday, but then that was a work of charity. Well, but mine is a work of charity too. . . . Our Tabernacle is to be the model of a holy – a very holy thing which it is right to think about on Sunday. Then it is to be made for a very charitable purpose."

Dora convinces herself with this argument, but remorse soon settles upon her, and she becomes conscious of the fearful sin she has committed.

This type of religious practice Dickens attacks in *Little Dorrit* in the person of Mrs. Clennam who, in widow's weeds, surrounded by pictures of the Plagues of Egypt, sits alone in her room with the Bible by her side,

1 A.L.O.E., pseudonym of Charlotte Maria Tucker (1821–93). Missionary in India and author of many evangelical stories for children.

PREPARING FOR SUNDAY

"Haste! put your playthings all away,
  To-morrow is the sabbath-day;
  Come! bring to me your Noah's Ark,
  Your pretty, tinkling music-cart;
  Because, my love, you must not play,
  But holy keep the sabbath-day."

From The Infant's Magazine, 1868.

A DICKENS EVANGELICAL

Mrs. Clennam on her "black, bier-like sofa". Detail from an illustration to
Little Dorrit.

brooding on her own righteousness and on the unrighteousness of others.
"Great need had the rigid woman of her mystical religion, veiled in gloom
and darkness, with lightnings of cursing, vengeance, and destruction,
flashing through the sable clouds." She sustains herself on an invalid's
diet of such luxuries as oysters and partridge and spiced negus, and prays
the while that her enemies may be put to the edge of the sword, consumed
by fire, smitten by plagues and leprosy, that their bones may be ground to
dust, and that they may be utterly exterminated. Her son remembers the
terrifying Sundays the family used to spend.

"There was the dreary Sunday of his childhood, when he sat with his hands
before him, scared out of his senses by a horrible tract which commenced
business with the poor child by asking him in its title, why he was going
to Perdition? – a piece of curiosity that he really in a frock and drawers
was not in a condition to satisfy – and which, for the further attraction of
his infant mind, had a parenthesis in every other line with some such hiccup-
ing reference as 'Ep. Thess. c. iii v. 6 & 7.' There was the sleepy Sunday

of his boyhood, when, like a military deserter, he was marched to chapel by a picquet of teachers three times a day, morally handcuffed to another boy; and when he would willingly have bartered two meals of indigestible sermon for another ounce or two of inferior mutton at his scanty dinner in the flesh. There was the interminable Sunday of his nonage; when his mother, stern of face and unrelenting of heart, would sit all day behind a bible – bound, like her own construction of it, in the hardest, barest, and straitest boards, with one dinted ornament on the cover like the drag of a chain, and a wrathful sprinkling of red upon the edges of the leaves – as if it, of all books, were a fortification against sweetness of temper, natural affection, and gentle intercourse. There was the resentful Sunday of a little later, when he sat glowering and glooming through the tardy length of the day, with a sullen sense of injury in his heart, and no more real knowledge of the beneficent history of the New Testament, than if he had been bred among idolaters."

Respectability, besides religious observance, also included a fastidious shrinking from all coarse physical facts, and in particular shielding the middle class female mind from such matters. G. M. Young styled it 'the Blush-to-the-Cheek-of-the-Young-Person business', referring to Dickens' Mr. Podsnap (in *Our Mutual Friend*), who epitomizes prosperous middle-class Victorian respectability at its worst.

"Mr. Podsnap was well to do, and stood very high in Mr. Podsnap's opinion. Beginning with a good inheritance, he had married a good inheritance, and had thriven exceedingly in the Marine insurance way, and was quite satisfied. He never could make out why everybody was not quite satisfied, and he felt conscious that he set a brilliant social example in being particularly well satisfied with most things, and, above all other things, with himself.

Mr. Podsnap's world was not a very large world, morally; no, nor even geographically: seeing that although his business was sustained upon commerce with other countries, he considered other countries, with that important reservation, a mistake, and of their manners and customs would conclusively observe, 'Not English!' when, PRESTO! with a flourish of the arm, and a flush of the face, they were swept away. Elsewise, the world got up at eight, shaved close at a quarter-past, breakfasted at nine, went to the City at ten, came home at half-past five, and dined at seven."

Literature, considered Mr. Podsnap, was an account of lives such as his, just as painting and sculpture should represent lives such as his, and music should express the same. The Podsnaps live in a sombre house furnished in a style of hideous solidity. "Everything was made to look as heavy as it could, and to take up as much room as possible." They have a daughter who is being very carefully brought up and kept uncontaminated from association with other people of her age.

"A certain institution in Mr. Podsnap's mind which he called 'the young person' may be considered to have been embodied in Miss Podsnap, his daughter. It was an inconvenient and exacting institution, as requiring everything in the universe to be filed down and fitted to it. The question about everything was, would it bring a blush into the cheek of the young person? And the inconvenience of the young person was, that, according to Mr. Podsnap, she seemed always liable to burst into blushes when there was no need at all. There appeared to be no line of demarcation between the young person's excessive innocence, and another person's guiltiest knowledge. Take Mr. Podsnap's word for it, and the soberest tints of drab, white, lilac, and grey, were all flaming red to this troublesome Bull of a young person."

In Podsnappery Dickens attacked the worst side of the Victorian middle class, the self-satisfied, prosperous respectability, that surrounded itself with solid, hideous possessions and thrust out of sight any matter that might be embarrassing or unpleasant. Podsnappery is what Matthew Arnold attacked as Philistinism.

7 · The Church

VICTORIAN England was religious. It was not merely that a great deal of thought was given to religious matters, and that feelings ran strong on religious topics, but that the customs of society were greatly affected by religious practices.

It might also be said that the Church during the Victorian period was to be seen at its best and its greatest. There was a spirit of ardent dedication, an awaking into life after the slothful days of the Georgians. The Victorian period is the age when we see men of the calibre of Newman labouring in industrial parishes; Canon Girdlestone fighting for the bettering of the lives of the agricultural workers in Devon. It is a time when people struggled to raise money to build new churches for the swarming populations of cities, and to put to rights the churches which the indifference of the older generation had allowed to tumble into ruin; when young women eagerly debated among themselves which they should put first, their home or their church duties, and took up work in the schools or among the poor of their parish. It is the time of the great clerical headmasters: Dr. Arnold at Rugby, George Ridding at Winchester, James Prince Lee at King Edward's, Birmingham (both of the latter two later becoming bishops of new industrial dioceses); a time of fine scholarship and of passionate religious controversy, of self-dedication and self-denial.

Over the form their religion should take the Victorians were fiercely

Chapter heading from *The Infant's Magazine,* 1868.

CONFIRMATION OF SCHOOLBOYS IN WESTMINSTER ABBEY

A very Anglican scene, combining the glories of mediaeval architecture, the emblems of national pride, and a conscious good taste in the avoidance of any ritualistic extremes. Engraving by Doré from *London,* 1872.

divided; the differences between the various denominations were matters of burning interest and often fierce antagonism. There was the Church of England – the Anglican church – the Established Church of the land which claimed to be the direct inheritor of the Christianity brought to its shores by St. Augustine in the 6th century. It had separated itself from Rome in the reign of Henry VIII, and had developed a more and more national character as the centuries had worn on. This was the religion of the sovereign (who was its supreme governor), of the ruling classes, and, at the beginning of the 19th century before dissent had lured away many from the churches, of the great majority. Its bishops and higher dignitaries were (and are) appointed by the sovereign in consultation with the Prime Minister, and no alteration may be made in the liturgy and conduct of the church services as laid down in the Book of Common Prayer in the reign of Elizabeth I. The relation between Church and State was to cause much anguish in the Victorian period, and was the cause of many Anglicans – of whom Newman was one – leaving their native church for Rome.

The Church of England was not financed by the State, though much of its income was derived from rates and tithes levied upon land that might well belong to a dissenter or a non-believer – a fact which gave rise to much bitterness and opposition.

Within the Anglican church there were parties that warred against each other as hotly as against any denomination outside their fold. They all subscribed to the Thirty Nine Articles of religion adopted by the church in Elizabeth's reign, and they all used the Book of Common Prayer, but in spite of this they might be of completely different climates of opinion. The Low Church party differed little in their theology from Methodists, while at the other extreme some members of the High Church party adopted most of the usages of the Roman Catholic Church.

Outside the Church of England were the Dissenters or Noncomformists: Quakers, Baptists, Methodists, Congregationalists. Some of these denominations had dissociated themselves from the established church long before; the Methodists were newly separated, as a result of Wesley's evangelizing in the previous century. But Wesley's influence extended far beyond those followers of his whom their contemporaries derisively had called methodists from the ordered piety of their lives. It affected those who never left the Church of England; it was responsible for the evangelical morality that was such a feature of Victorian England

and Victorian churchmanship; it brought a new seriousness into the lives of people who a generation before would have been content to be dissipated, worldly and frivolous.

The religious climate changed dramatically in the 19th century. The 18th century – apart from Wesley and his followers – had been generally sceptical, indifferent and cool. The aristocratic landowner, though he would desire that his cottagers should be regular churchgoers for the good of their morals, might be an unbeliever himself. Lord Melbourne, Queen Victoria's first Prime Minister, an aristocrat of the 18th century sort, acciden‑tally found himself the unwilling hearer of a rousing evangelical sermon about sin and its consequences, and exclaimed with much disgust as he left the church: "Things have come to a pretty pass when religion is allowed to invade the sphere of private life!" The typical clergyman of the pre‑evangelical period that we, say, meet in Jane Austen's novels, is a well‑bred, respectable, kindly man, playing an agreeable part in the social life of his neighbourhood. Such a man might feel great dislike for the more emotional forms of religion as practised by the followers of Wesley, who in their turn would attack the established church for its worldliness, indifference, and sloth.

Mr. Irwine in *Adam Bede*, which George Eliot set in 1799, is a clergyman of this old school, a gentle, humane man, attacked by the local Wesleyan preacher in a general statement concerning the Church clergy of the district:

"whom he described as men given up to the lusts of the flesh and the pride of life; hunting and shooting, and adorning their own houses; asking what shall we eat, and what shall we drink, and wherewithal shall we be clothed? – careless of dispensing the bread of life to their flocks, preaching at best but a carnal and soul‑benumbing morality, and trafficking in the souls of men by receiving money for discharging the pastoral office in parishes where they did not so much as look on the faces of the people more than once a year."

George Eliot describes Mr. Irwine with affection, admitting that he has no lofty aims, no theological enthusiasm, no serious alarm about the souls of his parishioners.

"He thought the custom of baptism more important than its doctrine, and that the religious benefits the peasant drew from the church where his fathers worshipped and the sacred piece of turf where they lay buried, were but slightly dependent on a clear understanding of the Liturgy or the sermon. Clearly the Rector was not what is called in these days an 'earnest' man; he was fonder of church history than of divinity, and had much more insight into men's characters than interest in their opinions; he was neither laborious, nor obviously self-denying, nor very copious in alms-giving, and his theology, you perceive, was lax...."

Mr. Irwine is a favourable example of the old type of clergyman. But there were many who were far less conscientious than he, plenty of parishes where church and parishioners were woefully neglected. Alexis de Tocqueville, when he came to England in 1833, questioned Lord Radnor on the current state of religion in England. Lord Radnor replied:

"Religion is running great risks at the moment due to the fault of its ministers. The clergy of the Established Church seem to do all in their power to alienate the goodwill of the people; it becomes the cynosure of many hatreds and I fear that in the end religion itself will suffer. Generally our clergy leads a regular life but it fulfils its duties lazily and without zeal. Here, for example, we have a clergyman who does not reside, his pretext being that his health does not permit him to do so. He lives in the neighbouring town leaving all the care of the parish to a poor devil encumbered with a young wife and six children, and to whom he gives perhaps only a tenth of his stipend. It is the same-in a great many places; the resident clergy are generally young people who take all the responsibilities of the apostolic ministry, but have barely enough to live on. Tithes are beginning to cause great hatred against the clergy. The number of Dissenters is rapidly increasing; sects are multiplying infinitely."

Adam Bede was written in 1859, and probably George Eliot had in mind the bigotry of Victorian evangelicals when she spoke warmly of Mr. Irwine's tolerance. The Victorian evangelicals – of whom we have already met a terrifying example in the person of Dickens' Mrs. Clennam, sitting meditating on her own uprightness and on the wickedness of those who are not of her way of thinking – were markedly severe on the opinions and behaviour of those with whom they found themselves in disagreement.

I will praise God with my voice; for I may praise Him, though I am but a little child.

A few years ago, and I was a little infant, and my tongue was dumb within my mouth:

And I did not know the great name of God, for my reason was not come unto me.

But now I can speak, and my tongue shall praise Him:

Hymns in prose for children
Mrs. Barbauld's book of praise, originally published in 1781, remained popular throughout the Victorian period. For thousands of Victorian children it was their first religious book. This page comes from an edition of 1863.

The evangelical movement which, as has been said, had such a profound effect on Victorian England, began with John Wesley.[1] He had preached up and down the land, striving to breathe a new spirit into the Church, to stir it out of its torpor, to bring religion to the lives of working men who had never before experienced it. It did this and more. It not only attracted thousands of men and women who, under the old system, would never have been reached by the Church, it also inspired those within the Church. Men grappled with the social evils that they saw about them; William Wilberforce denounced the slave trade; Lord Shaftesbury the appalling treatment of women and children employed in factories and mines. The clergy were fired with new spirit, the old, slack, 18th century ways were discarded, the hunting parson with his nightly three bottles of port became a thing of the past. Much attention was given to theological problems, to the better organization of the Church, to such matters as the redistribution of clerical incomes. The fervour that had originally stemmed from the teaching of Wesley and his adherents led men to question their beliefs. And having questioned them, many were to discard them, some to join the Roman Church – there was a great surge in this direction which Newman led in the 1840's – some to renounce religious belief altogether. No thinking men were *indifferent* to religion in the Victorian period; it was in the forefront of their minds, whether they practised it, or had decided after much inward conflict to abandon it.

Throughout the mid-Victorian age the evangelical movement was the strongest religious force. There were the direct descendants of Wesley, to be found in the Methodist church, by this time quite separated from the Church of England – though Wesley had never intended this should be so. Other Dissenters: Baptists, Quakers and Congregationalists, were touched by its fire. Within the Church of England was a group, known as the Low Church, of evangelical clergymen.

The beliefs of the evangelicals cut right across the divisions between one denomination and another. Socially, as will be discussed more fully later, there was a world of difference between a chapel-goer and a church-goer; in terms of what they believed there might be little to separate them. The evangelical religion was a very personal one, it laid great stress on the relation between an individual and God. For a man to be saved he had to recognize that he was a great sinner, to repent of his sins, and to experience

---

1 John Wesley (1703–91). Preacher and leader of Methodism. Became leader, while still at Oxford, of the "Methodist" society founded by his brother Charles, of young men who led a strict life of fasting and prayer. Travelled thousands of miles up and down Britain preaching the gospel.

conversion – that is, to realize that Christ had died for him personally. Only the individual himself could know whether he had experienced conversion and was "saved", no priest could give him any assurance on this point. Without conversion, the evangelicals held, good works and churchgoing were useless to a man's soul.

It was the very personal nature of evangelicalism that, paradoxically, drove so many away from it. Taught that religion was a matter of one's own conscience, men questioned their feelings, and might be driven to abandon their earlier beliefs. Evangelicals laid much stress on sin and repentance; on death and eternal punishment and on the literal interpretation of the Old Testament. It was they who insisted on treating Sunday, not as a day of rest on which one went to church, but as a day of savage prohibitions, and restrictions as elaborate as those laid down for the Jews. We have seen something of this in the last chapter.

There is a vast quantity of evangelical children's literature of the mid-Victorian period which emphasizes all these points. In many of them the child characters act as evangelists, urging those around them to repent

THE CHILD CONVERTING HER ELDERS
A favourite Victorian theme. This illustration of a little girl giving a tract to a sailor comes from *The Children's Friend,* 1866.

and be saved. "Has the Good Shepherd found *you*?" persistently asks the little girl in *A Peep Behind the Scenes*, Mrs. O. F. Walton's story of circus life which was much loved in the later decades of the last century. "Wash me, and I shall be whiter than show," says Nell, dying of consumption in *Whiter than Snow*, a popular, anonymous, story, and she teaches her drunkard father to repeat these words. Death plays a prominent part in all these books, and much eloquence is lavished on the behaviour of the dying person, and his uplifting utterances to those gathered round his bed.

Mrs. Sherwood[1] is one of the most extreme examples of the evangelical children's writers. She strongly believed in the edifying influence of deathbeds, and Henry, Lucy, and Emily Fairchild in her *History of the Fairchild Family* (written in three parts between 1818 and 1847) are taken to see not only corpses, but also to witness godly deaths, an experience which the children find terrifying for "death, even the death of those whose souls are redeemed, is a dreadful sight; for the sinful body struggles hard with it." On one memorable occasion they are shown the corpse of a murderer hanging in chains on a gibbet, to cure them of a tendency to quarrel.

To avoid hell, Mrs. Sherwood insisted, the child must learn as its first religious truth 'the awful doctrine of man's depravity'. Her teaching was stern indeed (though it is only fair to add that it is interspersed with much charming domestic detail about the home life of the little Fairchilds and their contemporaries). Henry Fairchild, who refuses to learn his Latin, is flogged and then sent to coventry by his entire family, and is only brought to his right mind by much godly conversation with a pious little boy who talks to him about everlasting burning, and death and corpses and worms and vaults and coffins. Little Susan, in *The History of Susan Gray* is told that if she goes to school she will learn to be good. "'Will you be content to leave off playing in the street, and will you give up your time to working and reading? Children who play in the streets with others, learn to lie and to swear, and perhaps to steal. They grow up to be idle, bold, bad men and women; and when they die, they go to a place where they live with devils in fire and brimstone and chains and darkness.'"

Deep interest in the deathbed, and the feeling of the importance of the

---

1 Mrs. Mary Martha Sherwood, née Butt (1775–1851). Author of many stories and tracts, among them *Little Henry and his Bearer* and *The History of Henry Milner*, familiar in evangelical households.

last words of the dying was by no means confined to the storybook. Noel
Annan in his book on Leslie Stephen tells an amusing story of a Dr.
Geldart who in the 1850's was Master of Trinity Hall, Cambridge. A
cleric of the old school, he only desired to be left in peace to enjoy his port
in the evening, but was beset by vigorous young colleagues who tried to
stir him out of his sloth, and by a formidable evangelical wife. The young
colleagues, in spite of everything, were fond of him, and scandalized Mrs.
Geldart by coming to visit him when he was dying, and cheering him so
successfully that he raised himself in bed and called for a bottle of port and
his fishing tackle. Mrs. Geldart lamented on how difficult it was for her
to get her husband into a fitting state of mind. "I don't know why it is, but I
can't get poor dear Charles to take any interest in the arrangements for his
funeral." As a good evangelical she waited anxiously for her husband's
last words which would indicate that his thoughts were fixed on higher
things. But he found it hard to take leave of the pleasures of the flesh.
When at last he felt himself gripped by the pangs of death, his mind turned
again to the convivialities which had meant so much to him during his
life. "You will let the undergraduates have some of the old sherry," he
gasped and fell back dead. Mrs. Geldart was so appalled that she called
for an autopsy, and was immensely relieved to hear that there was evidence
that the Master's mind had become clouded towards his death.

There are many examples of evangelicals in Victorian literature, with
pious exclamations on their lips and put their own advancement in their
hearts, like Dickens' unctuous hypocrite, Mr. Chadband, and Trollope's
Mr. Slope. The Anglo-Catholic clergy, curiously, seemed to escape this
sort of attack. The novelists were not scrupulous in the way they aroused
in their readers dislike for these characters; unpleasant physical characteristics were mixed up with pious utterances as though they were all part
and parcel of this sort of religious belief. So, Mr. Chadband is "a large
yellow man, with a fat smile, and a general appearance of having a good
deal of train oil in his system," and much given to heavy eating. Trollope's
Mr. Slope has lank red hair, a face the colour of bad quality beef, a spongy,
porous nose, and cold, clammy hands. Trollope's account of Mr. Slope's
religious views are fairer comment on this particular sort of Low Churchmanship.

"With Wesleyan-Methodists he has something in common, but his soul

DICKENS MOCKS EVANGELICAL PREACHING

Mr. Chadband lectures the Snagsby family and their servants on the nature of "terewth". An illustration from *Bleak House.*

trembles in agony at the iniquities of the Puseyites. His aversion is carried to things outward as well as inward. His gall rises at a new church with a high pitched roof; a full-breasted black silk waistcoat is with him a symbol of Satan; and a profane jest-book would not, in his view, more foully desecrate the church seat of a Christian, than a book of prayer printed with red letters, and ornamented with a cross on the back. Most active clergy-men have their hobby, and Sunday observances are his. Sunday, however, is a word which never pollutes his mouth – it is always 'the Sabbath'. The 'desecration of the Sabbath,' as he delights to call it, is to him meat and drink:– he thrives upon that as policemen do on the general evil habits of the community. . . . To him the revelation of God appears only in that one law given for Jewish observance. . . . To him the New Testament is comparatively of little moment, for from it can be drawn no fresh authority for that dominion which he loves to exercise over at least a seventh part of man's allotted time here below."

A penetrating study of the evangelical character occurs in Trollope's account of Mrs. Bolton in *John Caldigate*. Mrs. Bolton is determined to prevent her daughter Hester from marrying:

"She was so afraid of the world, the flesh, and the devil, that she would fain shut up her child so as to keep her from the reach of all evil. Vowed celibacy was abominable to her, because it was the resource of the Roman Catholics; and because she had been taught to believe that convent-walls were screens for hiding unheard-of wickedness. But yet, on behalf of her child, she desired seclusion from the world, fancying that so, and so only, might security be ensured. Superstition was as strong with her as with any self-flagellated nun. Fasting, under that name, she held in abhorrence. But all sensual gratifications were wicked in her sight. She would allow all home indulgences to her daughter, each under some separate plea, – constrained to do so by excessive love; but she did so always in fear and trembling, lest she was giving some foothold to Satan."

Despite her mother, Hester insists on marrying John Caldigate. Mrs. Bolton laments and tells her that John Caldigate is unregenerate, and therefore a man of the world, and therefore a disciple of Mammon, that her daughter cannot touch pitch without being defiled, and will be dragged down to the pit with him. She attends the wedding as a stranger, dressed in mourning and deeply veiled, praying "not, it is to be feared, that John Caldigate might be a good husband to her girl, but that he, as he made his way downward to things below, might not drag her darling with him."

Disaster later follows from this marriage; it seems that John Caldigate has already a wife in Australia. Mrs. Bolton comes to Hester and tells her that she must abandon him and come back to the family home. But Hester is adamant. She says that she has prayed for guidance, and that God has directed her as to her future life. But though the mother is not convinced (for, as Trollope says, those who direct their children to pray for guidance never expect that guidance will be given contrary to the parent's wishes), she hardly knew "how to mount to higher ground, so as to seem to speak from a more exalted eminence."

Many evangelicals, in fact and in fiction, found themselves in difficulties through their insistence on this personal relation with God, and were not prepared for the fact that it might lead those that they loved to go in a direction that they least expected. William Wilberforce was a fervent evangelical; of his four sons, three joined the Roman Church. Sir James Stephen was another; his son, Leslie,[1] renounced Holy Orders and became an agnostic.

Edmund Gosse,[2] in *Father and Son*, has left a record of an upbringing as a member of the Plymouth Brethren, a Protestant sect of extreme strict^ ness. For much of his childhood the little Edmund was kept at home, the constant companion of his widowed father, denied most of the things that are usually reckoned to be childish pleasures. There was one occasion when the servants felt so sorry for him on Christmas Day that they smuggled him a slice of the plum pudding which they had made for themselves against the wishes of Mr. Gosse. But the child's conscience smote him, and he turned it away.

After he was ten, however, a spirit of resistance began to well up within him. A wealthy family of Baptists asked him "to tea and games". Mr. Gosse was very doubtful about the advisability of this. Though the pleasures might be innocent in themselves, they might give an appetite for yet more subversive dissipations. So he summoned Edmund upstairs, that they might "lay the matter before the Lord."

"We did so, kneeling side by side, with our backs to the window and our foreheads pressed upon the horsehair cover of the small, coffin^like sofa. My Father prayed aloud, with great fervour, that it might be revealed to me, by the voice of God, whether it was or was not the Lord's will that I should attend the Browns' party. My Father's attitude seemed to me to be hardly fair, since he did not scruple to remind the Deity of various objections to a life of pleasure and of the snakes that lie hidden in the grass of evening parties. It would have been more scrupulous, I thought, to give no sort of hint of the kind of answer he desired and expected.

"It will be justly said that my life was made up of very trifling things, since I have to confess that this incident of the Browns' invitation was one of its landmarks. As I knelt, feeling very small, by the immense bulk of my Father, there gushed through my veins like a wine the determination to rebel. Never before, in all these years of my vocation, had I felt my resistance take precisely this definite form. We rose presently from the sofa, my fore^ head and the backs of my hands still chafed by the texture of the horsehair, and we faced one another in the dreary light. My Father, perfectly confident

2 Sir Edmund Gosse (1849–1928). Poet, critic, man of letters.

───────

1 Sir Leslie Stephen (1832–1904). Philosopher and man of letters, first editor of the Dictionary of National Biography. Father of Virginia Woolf.

FAMILY PRAYERS IN AN EVANGELICAL HOUSEHOLD
On the wall hangs a family pledge of temperance. This and the illustration on
p. 157 were printed as "outline drawing lessons" in *The Children's Friend*, 1881–3.

in the success of what had really been a sort of incantation, asked me in a
loud wheedling voice, 'Well, and what is the answer our Lord vouch-
safes?' I said nothing, and so my Father, more sharply, continued, 'We
have asked Him to direct you to a true knowledge of His Will. We have
desired Him to let you know whether it is, or is not, in accordance with His
wishes that you should accept this invitation from the Browns.' He
positively beamed down at me; he had no doubt of the reply. He was
already, I believe, planning some little treat to make up to me for the material
deprivation. But my answer came, in the high-piping accents of despair:
'The Lord says I may go to the Browns.' My Father gazed at me in speech-
less horror. He was caught in his own trap, and though he was certain that

the Lord had said nothing of the kind, there was no road open for him but just sheer retreat."

A great feature of the Victorian evangelicals was their horror of the Roman Catholic Church. They saw in it all that was evil, blasphemous and corrupt, they accused it of attempts to ensnare innocent Protestants by the foulest of means. Mrs. Sherwood in *The Nun* (1833) recounted fearful practices that went on in a convent where nuns were entombed in dungeons for years on end, for holding wrongful opinions. In a gift book published by the Religious Tract Society in the 1850's we are given the "true" story of a girl who goes as a governess to a Roman Catholic family, marked out – though she does not know it – as a possible convert to the Roman faith. There she meets a delightful man who suggests that he will marry her if she renounces her Protestant faith. She agrees, but at the ceremony of recantation she sees the man she hopes to marry – in the vestments of a priest. Raving mad, she falls to the ground. "Her feelings had received too deep a shock, and the admired and courted girl was a confirmed imbecile." "'Her soul is saved,' said the Jesuit priest, who had played his cruel part so well; 'what matters the perishing body?'"

Hundreds of evangelical books for children took up this theme, pointing out the snares that Rome laid for the unwary, describing with abhorrence Romish customs (such as those which Trollope's Mrs. Bolton deplored) and the disgraceful way that Roman Catholic countries neglected the Sabbath.

Edmund Gosse describes the unreasoning horror with which a child, brought up in this way, viewed Rome. No one had been more ardent than he, he said, in flaming denunciations of the Papacy, for if there was one institution that he loathed as a child "it was what we invariably spoke of as 'the so-called Church of Rome.'" In later years he met plenty of stout Protestants who saw the hand of the Jesuits in every public and private misfortune, but they were mild compared to the spirit of the Gosses and their kind in the 1850's.

They spoke of Rome, he said, in the most violent terms, using 17th century terms of abuse of a sort that it would now be hardly decent to use. When, as a little boy, he thought of the Pope, he used to shut his eyes and clench his fists, though he had little idea of what a pope might be. Any disorder in any part of Italy the Gosses, father and son, welcomed as a sign that liberty and light was at last breaking upon a God-forsaken country.

TRADITIONAL ENGLISH FEAR OF THE ROMAN CHURCH

This was intensified in 1850 when Pope Pius IX (caricatured above as trying to break into the English church) established a new hierarchy in England. *Punch*, from which this cartoon is taken, directed many attacks against the Papists and "their Anglican apes, the Puseyites".

"As a child, whatever I might question, I never doubted the turpitude of Rome. I do not think I had formed any idea whatever of the character or pretensions or practices of the Catholic Church, or indeed of what it consisted, or its nature, but I regarded it with a vague terror as a wild beast, the only good point about it being that it was very old and was soon to die."

These then were the evangelicals, and some of their opinions. After the first generation of men such as Wilberforce and Shaftesbury, it was not, on the whole, a type of religion that appealed to the intellectual mind, and many intellectuals brought up in it as children deserted it later in life. There were, as has been said, evangelicals within the Church of England as well as among the Dissenters.

There was a second school of thought within the Church which came to be known as the Broad Church movement. Men like Thomas Arnold and his biographer A. P. Stanley were not so much interested in the dramatic saving of the individual soul as in the moral and educational influence of the Church upon the nation. They valued the Church of England because it was a *national* church with a dignified liturgy. They were not exacting. Theologically speaking, they thought that everybody should interpret the doctrines of the Church to suit himself, so that the Church of England could contain all shades of belief.

The third Anglican party was the High Church party. While the Low Church party stressed the Protestant, reformed nature of the church (the aspect which it had taken on after the break with Rome in Henry VIII's time), and the Broad Church stressed its national character, High Churchmen valued its ancient origins, the bishops linked by laying-on of hands with Christ himself, the sacraments which Christ had ordained. The Oxford Movement of the 1830's began as a movement to remind the Church of England of this aspect of its history. To this end, Newman, Keble, and Pusey, all of them at that time fellows of Oxford colleges, issued their famous Tracts for the Times, the first of which appeared in 1833, emphasizing the divine origins of the Church, and the great danger that it was in from domination by the state.

Newman was to find himself in increasing difficulties. He came to realize that the church that he sought, a divine church that spoke with an infallible voice and that was linked with no secular state, was not to be found within the Church of England, and in 1845 he left it to join the Church of Rome, taking with him a multitude of others. Newman's departure and the mass secessions that followed it rocked and shook the Anglican Church in the mid-years of the century, and there is much reference to it in the literature of the period. Trollope's Mr. Arabin, who was to become Dean of Barchester, was a High Church clergyman who at Oxford had taken up cudgels on the side of the Tractarians, and had "sat at the feet of the great Newman." In *Barchester Towers* there is reference to the way that he too nearly followed Newman to Rome, though after much inward conflict he decided in the end to remain an Anglican.

Keble and Pusey, who stayed within the Church of England, were men of a different sort. Keble was a gentle, spiritual man, much loved, but too lacking in forcefulness to be a leader. Pusey was a man of stern, even grim

THE ROMAN CHURCH LURES RITUALISTS TO THEIR
DESTRUCTION

This cartoon of 1869, expressing Low Church hatred and suspicion of the High
Church movement, shows Pope Pius IX followed by Manning and other bishops
of the Roman church sliding on thin ice. *Punch* watches, horrified, while High
Church clergy on the opposite bank flock to join in the dangerous game.

asceticism, infinitely harsh towards himself; he even took a vow never to
smile again except at children. Pusey and his followers introduced into
their services practices that appalled the Low Churchmen – candles and
vestments, for instance, most of which are taken for granted today. They
advocated private confession, founded religious communities. They were
known sometimes as Ritualists, sometimes as Puseyites, or more court-
eously as Anglo-Catholics, and their activities were denounced with
hysterical fury in many quarters, though as the century progressed these
were to be accepted as standard practice, and brought dignity and reverence
into churches which had seen deplorable neglect and indifference.

Richard Jefferies in *Hodge and his Master* spoke of some of the changes
that had come about with an energetic new vicar. His predecessor had
been a man of whom it was said, "he was a very good sort of man: he never
interfered with anybody or anything." The new vicar introduced a choir,
doing away with the old motley collection of village instrumentalists. He
brought colours into the hangings and decoration of the church, and put
flowers and candlesticks on the altar. He held early morning celebrations

of communion, he left the church open all day for private prayer. He reminded the people of Lent and Easter, festivals and saints' days, and emphasized the importance of the communion service. He saw to it that the district was visited, that no cottage was left neglected. All this was an immense change from the days when the gentry dozed peacefully in high boxed-in pews while the preacher in black gown and white bands thumped the red velvet cushion on his pulpit during the lengthy course of his forty minute sermon, which with the Litany and the Psalms formed the main part of Sunday worship.

Samuel Cooper Scott has left recollections of his father's church in the 1840's in the days before the influence of the Ritualists had made itself felt. Burials still took place within the church itself. "I have seen shallow graves dug in the middle aisle, and the coffin deposited within a very little distance of the pavement over which the people passed to their places on the following Sunday . . . the earth was thrown up against the pew doors." His father preached from the three-decker pulpit which was a relic of previous centuries, consisting of a pulpit, reading desk, and clerk's desk where the parish clerk sat and gave out the hymns. The girls from the local charity school sat in their uniform in ascending seats on either side of the organ. Round the church were deep galleries, very dark owing to the lowness of the roof. On each side of the pulpit were a number of benches without backs which faced down the church, here sat the poor who after the service would each receive a loaf of bread. The vicarage family sat in a large square pew with a book board down the middle round which they stood to sing and knelt to pray.

All this was to be swept away by the zeal of the reformers, who in their enthusiasm sometimes went too far and destroyed architectural features which later generations have mourned. Their innovations were ill-received by the Low Churchmen of their time, and practices which are now accepted unquestioningly were fought over with savage ferocity. There were riots in Exeter when Bishop Phillpotts instructed his clergy to preach wearing a surplice, and one rector lived for a time with the windows of the rectory barred and alarm bells on the shutters.

Lady Charlotte Guest commented in her diary on what she considered was dangerously Popish behaviour on the part of the local clergyman.

"Feb. 15, 1850. We find a great sensation produced at Canford by Mr.

Ponsonby's proceedings. He had services in the little Mortuary Chapel on Ash Wednesday. . . . His sermon was partly on Confirmation, partly on Baptism, and Mr. Ball represents it to have been very Popish. But what shocked all present was a print on the little altar of a crucifix and our Saviour upon it and two high candlesticks on the sides. All his demeanour too, and his turning to this altar and from the people when in prayer startled them very much. It has grieved me, I cannot say how deeply. The more so, as I fear I can do nothing to rescue our people from the contamination of witnessing practices which must tend to break down the feeling against the Papacy, at least in its ceremonials. I was much awake thinking over all this."

Though much in the Anglican church was reformed during the Victorian period, the clergy still remained what they always had been – gentlemen, drawn from the ranks of the upper classes. It was this that made them so markedly distinct from the Dissenting clergy. In 1892, P. Anderson Graham in *The Rural Exodus* made this point. The Anglican clergyman, he said, was usually a gentleman by birth, very likely to be a relative of the squires, at any rate a man who had been to Oxford or Cambridge. He depended for moral and material support upon the gentry of the neighbourhood, he had the same friends, the same amusements. The Nonconformist minister came from humbler origins altogether. Instead of dining with the squire he went out to tea with the tenant. On Sundays you would find in the church the squire, his household, servants, his principal tenants and the officials of the estate. In the chapel would gather "ungenteel" farmers, artisans, shopkeepers, and a sprinkling of "free" labourers (i.e. those who did not depend upon the squire). The Dissenting minister was almost always a keen and aggressive Radical, said Graham. He would not be a sportsman, and would be indifferent to such matters as fishing, shooting, cricket, and hunting, and other upper-class diversions in which the Church of England clergy often took a keen interest.

The working man too identified the Anglican clergy with the gentry, and the farm labourer often thought bitterly of the parson and the squire as being in league to keep wages low and grind the faces of the poor. A pamphlet written by a farm labourer in 1884 with the title *The Position of the Agricultural Labourer*, inveighs against this alliance:

"The parsons, my friends, have been prudent people, they are even to a

FAMILY CHURCH-GOING
From *The Children's Friend* (1881–83).

certain extent slaves of their rich patrons, the lords and squires, and therefore have stood by them as they hardly dare stand up for you; and of course
a good many of them are intimately bound up with the landed interest,
and of course are, and ever will be, against your rising out of your bonds."

The pamphleteer says that he knows some of the clergy are good wishers
to the working classes, but that they dare not speak out. He appreciates that
many clergy are generous givers of broth and such like, but he wants the
labouring man to have enough to do without such charity which makes
the people "more slavish than they would be if the case was otherwise."
   Kingsley's gamekeeper in *Yeast* makes this same point, as has been described in chapter five. Of the vicar he says that "'the poor don't understand
him, nor he them. He is too learned, sir, and saving your presence, too fond

of his Prayer-book.'" He goes on to say that the cottagers all believe the parsons have to be careful about how they speak to the squire. "'How else are they to get a farthing for schools, or coal-subscriptions, or lying-in societies, or lending libraries, or penny clubs? If they spoke their minds to the great ones, sir, how could they keep the parish together?'"

In the world of Trollope's Barsetshire, as seen in the six novels generally known as the Chronicles of Barsetshire – *The Warden, Barchester Towers, Doctor Thorne, Framley Parsonage, The Small House at Allington* and *The Last Chronicle of Barset*, problems such as these are not apparent. The studies of the Church of England made in these novels are popularly held to be a reflection of the state of affairs in the mid-Victorian period, but much is omitted. None of the burning controversies that flared up during that time, none of the agonized doubt, are brought in. Nor are social problems dwelt upon; here it is accepted that the clergy and squirearchy are in close connection and no one thinks the worse of them for it.

Trollope shows something of the antagonism between High and Low Church parties in the struggle between Mrs. Proudie, the bishop's wife, with the bishop's chaplain, Mr. Slope, against some of the clergy of the diocese, but this, as Trollope presents it, is seen to be more a struggle between personalities than between one set of opinions and another. Mrs. Proudie being an evangelical has strong views about Sunday travel, about whist being played in the bishop's palace, and about the necessity of Sunday schools (which she terms Sabbath-day schools). On the first occasion that she meets Archdeacon Grantley, who is a wealthy clergyman of the old school, she catechizes him about how such matters are handled in the diocese. "'Sabbath travelling'" the Archdeacon says furiously to his wife, referring to the Proudies and Mr. Slope, "'these are the sort of men who will ruin the Church of England, and make the profession of a clergyman disreputable. It is not the dissenters or the papists that we should fear, but the set of canting, low-bred hypocrites who are wriggling their way among us!'" This objection of the Archdeacon's to the Proudies and the Low Church party – that they are low-bred – is the objection of the Archdeacon alone, and does not reflect the feeling between High Church and Low Church generally at that time.

But in his portraits of Dean Arabin, Mr. Harding, and Mr. Crawley, Trollope does show the serious intellectual character and the unworld-liness that the Anglican Church could achieve. This, coming from a man who so well appreciated worldly motives in the church as elsewhere, is a tribute to the Church of that time. Mr. Crawley, a dedicated scholar and a conscientious priest, labours among the brickmakers of Hoggle End in abject poverty, disregarding his own needs and those of his family, and Dean Arabin stands loyally beside him through his troubles, accepting unresentfully the rebuffs that Mr. Crawley throws at him in his bitterness and despair.

It is in *The Warden*, perhaps, that Trollope best reflects the controversies and moods of the mid-Victorian Church. Here we are shown the battle that rages over the ancient almshouses of Hiram's Hospital in Barchester. Did the founder intend that the warden should draw from it a salary of £800 while the daily allowance of the ancient bedesmen who inhabit the hospital remains at one shilling and fourpence a day? The affair goes beyond Barchester, the national newspapers take it up and thunder about the iniquities of the case, while Mr. Harding, the hospital's warden, gentle, unworldly, conscientious, droops in the storm that whirls around him. The redistribution of incomes within the Church was one of the reforms that was brought about during the Victorian period and was hotly debated, and Trollope is at his most convincing here in his treatment of the motives that activate the warring parties.

The Victorian period, as has been said, saw much religious strife, and one of the saddest results of the divisions between the Established Church and the Dissenters was that it delayed for years the bringing in of a system for national education. The Church of England insisted that theirs should be the dominant influence in any such system; the Dissenters challenged this, and the 1843 scheme for the education of child factory workers was overthrown.

The enmity between Established Church and Dissenters ran high in those early years. We get some feeling of the strength of the dislike from the journal of the Rev. John Skinner, rector of Camerton in Somerset, who died in 1839. He refers to Wesley as an "ambitious adventurer", and talks about the preaching of his followers as "the crude undigested effusion of a cobbler or collier". He could not understand why members of his congregation should prefer to listen to this than follow "the beautiful service of our Liturgy." He also felt strongly that these uneducated, unlettered followers of Wesley did much damage among the people to whom they preached, and quotes instances where he has found them gathered

"WHO SHALL EDUCATE? OR, OUR BABES IN THE WOOD"
Punch in a cartoon of 1853 shows High Church and Dissent battling over church
schools.
"There the little children wander, while in mortal combat yonder
  Those who call themselves their guides for the mastery are fighting."

round the bedside of a dying man, terrifying him with their talk of hellfire
and eternal damnation.

George Eliot in *Adam Bede* on the other hand gives a very sympathetic
picture of the early Methodists. As in Skinner's Camerton, Wesley's
message is carried round by working men to working men, but the preaching
here is not so crude and we see the attraction that the movement held for
those who felt that the Church of England was for the gentry, not for them,
and that its clergy were lukewarm and uninspired. Dinah Morris, the
young Methodist preacher, looks, to the eye of the young squire at least,
like a St. Catherine in Quaker dress, and speaks to her gatherings of cottagers
and labourers, not so much of brimstone and everlasting flames as "of
the joys that were in store for the penitent, and . . . the divine peace and love
with which the soul of the believer is filled." Nor with Dinah does it end
with preaching; she is ready at an instant's call to nurse the sick, comfort

the bereaved, and pray with the dying. Her relations with the rector are very cordial; he does not strive to have her put out of the parish, though some of his parishioners are indignant that he countenances Methodists. Nor does she denounce him as an idle shepherd and a dumb dog as other members of her society have done.

Adam Bede refers to the state of affairs in 1799, Skinner was writing about the 1830's. Methodism by the mid-century was far more highly organized, preaching was no longer a matter of "crude effusions" by cobblers and colliers; there was an educated and ordained ministry. Methodism, and indeed all Nonconformism had become respectable. George Eliot in *The Mill on the Floss* sets down the views of the worthy inhabitants of St. Oggs, a provincial town in the 1830's. The days had gone by, to their mind, when preachers could shake the souls of men and induce them to change their faith. In these sober days nobody expected to be converted, and congregations had forgotten the schisms of earlier years, the disagree-ments that drove men to leave a church, and the fervour that won them over to another. Dissent now was something that one inherited, and the Church of England man only thought of it contemptuously as "a foolish habit that clung greatly to families in the grocery and chandlering lines, though not incompatible with prosperous wholesale dealing."

St. Oggs was not alone in associating a man's religion with his social class. De Tocqueville had noted it when he was investigating the state of religion in England in the 1830's. In reply to the Frenchman's question about the causes of change of religion, an Englishman replied that when a family became rich it left the Dissenters to join the Established Church. "It is a way of entering the bosom of the high aristocracy, or at least of rubbing shoulders with it. Then one finds oneself in fine churches where there are always carpets, comfortable pews, well-dressed people and well-educated preachers." But on the reverse side of this, de Tocqueville was told, "the poor man who is born in the bosom of the Established Church, is made uneasy by this very splendour; his feeling of inferiority takes him to a church where he finds his like in the congregation, and in the preacher a man less superior to himself and one who can say things within his grasp. A great many poor men . . . leave the Established Church for these reasons."

Matthew Arnold, writing in 1869, was another who identified chapel-going with tradesmen, as has already been mentioned in the previous chapter. Like the St. Oggs churchgoers he appeared to regard Dissent "as a foolish habit that clung greatly to families in the grocery and chandlering lines."

Mrs. Oliphant in *Salem Chapel* drew a very apt picture of a Dissenting community – some of whom we have already met in chapter 5 – and of the minister that served it. The exact brand of Dissent that Salem Chapel practises is not specified, though she admitted herself to having taken the details from the Free Church of Scotland as she knew it in Liverpool, and said that the workings of this were not unlike those of other Noncomformist bodies. But it is in her study of the Salem Chapel flock that the great merit of the book lies, rather than in the details of their beliefs. The description of the drab appearance of the chapel and its surroundings is in itself convincing.

"[The chapel] stood in a narrow strip of ground, just as the little houses which flanked it on either side stood in their gardens, except that the enclosure of the chapel was flowerless and sombre. . . . On either side of this little tabernacle were the humble houses – little detached boxes, each two storeys high, each fronted by a little flowerpot – clean, respectable, meagre, little habitations, which contributed most largely to the ranks of the congregation in the chapel. The big houses opposite, which turned their

AN EARLY VICTORIAN CHAPEL
From an edition of 1849 of Isaac Watts' *Divine and Moral Songs for Children*.

backs and staircase windows to the street took little notice of the humble Dissenting community."

Mrs. Oliphant dissects very neatly the class difference and the class feeling between the Anglican and the Dissenting clergyman. Mr. Wentworth, the Anglican, and Mr. Vincent of Salem chapel, are the same age, wear much the same clerical clothes, and are both good-looking young men. "How was it, then, that so vast a world of difference and separation lay between them?" For one moment Mr. Vincent thinks it is because of his enlightened faith, and feels himself persecuted. But he knows in his heart that this is not really so, it is in their outward circumstances that they are so different. "A poor widow's son, educated at [a Dissenting college], and an English squire's son, public school and university bred, cannot begin on the same level." So Mr. Vincent, longing for more congenial company than that of the small shopkeepers who form his congregation, has to accept

PREACHING THE GOSPEL
A bible reader at a night refuge for the destitute. Engraving by Doré (*London,* 1872).

that his Anglican counterpart is on easy terms of friendship with people
of the town whom he would like to know, but can only watch wistfully.
So the complicated English class structure invaded the religious life of
Victorian England too.

But it must not be forgotten that there were hundreds of thousands of
Victorians whom religion never touched at all. Few of the town-dwelling
poor had contact with religion. The number of churches was quite
inadequate to deal with the multitudes that by the beginning of Victoria's
reign were swarming into the new manufacturing cities. As the century
wore on great efforts were made to build new churches to grapple with this
problem, and devoted clergy gave up their lives to labour in slum parishes.
New sees were established, Manchester and Liverpool among them, to
serve new concentrations of population; missions, charities, schools were
founded to bring Christian education into the lives of the industrial poor.
But the problem was too great; inevitably the great majority of the city
dwellers were remote from the influence of church or chapel. The original
for Jo, the crossing-sweeper in *Bleak House* who "don't know nothink"
was a boy of 14 whose cross-examination in court on January 8, 1850 was
reported as follows:

Alderman : Well, do you know what you are about? Do you know what
an oath is?
Boy : No.
Alderman : Can you read?
Boy : No.
Alderman : Do you ever say your prayers?
Boy : No, never.
Alderman : Do you know what prayers are?
Boy : No.
Alderman : Do you know what God is?
Boy : No.
Alderman : Do you know what the devil is?
Boy : I've heard of the devil, but I don't know him.
Alderman : What do you know?
Boy : I knows how to sweep the crossings.
Alderman : And that's all?
Boy : That's all. I sweeps a crossing.

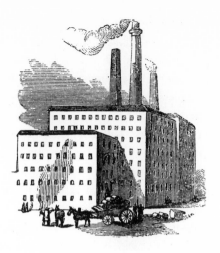

8 · Cities and Industry

THE Victorians inherited towns totally inadequate for the growth of population and the expansion of industry that had come about since the end of the 18th century. They had to grapple with gross overcrowding, with completely inadequate social facilities, and with the popular belief – so strong in the English and particularly so at that time – in the sacredness of private property even when it cut right against the public interest. They found themselves with cities where the poor were housed worse than animals, with great tracts of industrial land scattered haphazard with factories and slums, where there was no proper drainage, water, policing, or schools, and little or no system of local government to organize these. They left towns laid out in much the same pattern as we see today, with public offices, hospitals, schools, sewerage and water, mostly provided in the first instances by local rather than national effort.

A town such as Manchester, which had been insignificant until industry gave it a new importance in the 18th century, found itself in peculiar difficulties. It was overwhelmed by the pressure of the rapidly increasing numbers of its people, who poured into the city to find work in the mills when the new machinery put an end to what they could earn by hand in

Chapter heading from *The Infant's Magazine,* 1868.

their own cottages. These people, fresh from the country, new to city life, huddled wherever they could find shelter.

Very often they brought country practices with them; they did not see why they should not continue to keep a pig or a donkey, even though this now meant that the pig should share the cellar where the family lived. The city grew haphazard; there was no legislation to control the sprawl of one-room dwellings that crouched in the neighbourhood of Manchester's mills, with no streets, no drainage, no water. Engels[1] spoke of these areas in 1844 as "a planless, knotted, chaos of houses, more or less on the verge of uninhabitableness." He described families living in huts with earth floors, cellars which had to be bailed out every morning, pigs penned up or wandering down the unpaved lanes, families sharing their cellar rooms with horses, donkeys, or chickens. "Privies are so rare here that they are either filled up every day, or are too remote for most of the inhabitants to use. How can people wash when they have only the dirty Irk water at hand, while pumps and water pipes can be found in decent parts of the city alone?"

One of the best pictures of Manchester at about this time is given by de Tocqueville:

"An undulating plain, or rather a collection of little hills. Below the hills a narrow river (the Irwell) which flows slowly to the Irish sea. Two streams (the Medlock and the Irk) wind through the uneven ground and after a thousand bends flow into the river. Three canals made by man unite their tranquil, lazy waters at the same point. On this watery land, which nature and art have contributed to keep damp, are scattered palaces and hovels . . .

"Thirty or forty factories rise on the tops of the hills I have just described. Their six stories tower up; their huge enclosures give notice from afar of the centralization of industry. The wretched dwellings of the poor are scattered haphazard around them. Round them stretches land uncultivated but without the charm of rustic nature, and still without the amenities of a town. The soil has been taken away, scratched and torn up in a thousand places, but it is not yet covered with the habitations of men. The land is given over to industry's use. The roads which connect the still disjointed

1 Friedrich Engels (1820–95). German socialist, associated with Karl Marx. He was sent to work in his father's factory near Manchester in 1842; his *Condition of the Working Class in England in 1844* is one of the most valuable social documents of the time.

THE LAMBETH GAS WORKS

This engraving by the French illustrator, Doré, conveys something of the horror
with which many Victorians regarded industry and factory life.

limbs of the great city, show, like the rest, every sign of hurried or unfinished work; the incidental activity of a population bent on gain, which seeks to amass gold so as to have everything else all at once, and, in the interval, mistrusts the niceties of life. Some of these roads are paved, but most of them are full of ruts and puddles into which foot or carriage wheel sinks deep. Heaps of dung, rubble from buildings, putrid, stagnant pools are found here and there among the houses and over the bumpy, pitted surfaces of the public places. No trace of surveyor's rod or spirit-level. Amid this noisome labyrinth, this great sombre stretch of brickwork, from time to time one is astonished by the sight of fine stone buildings with Corinthian columns. It might be a medieval town, with the marvels of the 19th century in the middle of it. But who could describe the interiors of these quarters set apart, homes of vice and poverty, which surround the huge palaces of industry and clasp them in their hideous folds? On ground below the level of the river and overshadowed on every side by immense workshops, stretches marshy land which widely spaced muddy ditches can neither drain nor cleanse. Narrow, twisting roads lead down to it. They are lined with one-storey houses whose ill-fitting planks and broken windows show them up, even from a distance, as the last refuge a man might find between poverty and death. None the less, the wretched people reduced to living in them can still inspire jealousy of their fellow beings. Below some of their miserable dwellings is a row of cellars to which a sunken corridor leads. Twelve to fifteen human beings are crowded pell-mell into each of these damp repulsive holes.

"The fetid, muddy waters, stained with a thousand colours by the factories they pass, of one of the streams I mentioned before, wander slowly round this refuge of poverty. They are nowhere kept in place by quays; houses are built haphazard on their banks. Often from the top of their steep banks one sees an attempt at a road opening cut through the debris of earth, and the foundations of some houses or the recent ruins of others. It is the Styx of this new Hades.

"Look up, and all around this place you will see the huge palaces of industry. You will hear the noise of furnaces, the whistle of steam. These vast structures keep air and light out of the human habitations which they dominate; they envelop them in perpetual fog; here is the slave, there the master; there the wealth of some, here the poverty of most; there the organized effort of thousands produce, to the profit of one man, what society has not yet learnt to give. Here the weakness of the individual seems more feeble and helpless even than in the middle of a wilderness; here the effects, there the causes.

"A sort of black smoke covers the city. The sun seen through it is a disc without rays. Under this half daylight 300,000 human beings are cease-lessly at work. A thousand noises disturb this damp, dark labyrinth, but they are not all the ordinary sounds one hears in great cities.

"The footsteps of a busy crowd, the crunching wheels of machinery, the shriek of steam from boilers, the regular beat of the looms, the heavy rumble of carts, these are the noises from which you can never escape in the sombre half-light of these streets. You will never hear the clatter of hoofs as the rich man drives back home or out on expeditions of pleasure. Never the gay shouts of people amusing themselves, or music heralding a holiday. You will never see smart folk strolling at leisure in the streets, or going out on innocent pleasure parties in the surrounding country. Crowds are ever hurrying this way and that in the Manchester streets, but their footsteps are brisk, their looks pre-occupied, and their appearance sombre and harsh. Day and night the city echoes with street noises. But it is heavily loaded wagons lumbering slowly.

"From this foul drain the greatest stream of human industry flows out to fertilize the whole world. From this filthy sewer pure gold flows. Here humanity attains its most complete development and its most brutish; here civilization works its miracles, and civilized man is turned back almost into a savage."

De Tocqueville in this account of Manchester gives an impression of a people sacrificed to a new idol, the Moloch of industry, a devouring monster which exacts all the labour from them it can, and then tosses them aside to die; a monster spreading its tentacles over the countryside, blacken-ing and killing where it touches. Dickens describes this terrifying aspect of the new industrial age in *The Old Curiosity Shop*, published in 1841, some six years after de Tocqueville had given his impression of Manchester. Nell and her grandfather are fleeing through the midland Black Country, trying to escape their pursuers. The industrial landscape takes on the hideous aspect of a nightmare. They wander through towns shrouded in smoke, noisy with the clank of hammers beating upon iron, and the roar of busy streets, where the passers-by are too preoccupied even to spare them

THE BLACK COUNTRY ROUND WOLVERHAMPTON
Illustrated London News, 1866.

a glance. "Some frowned, some smiled, some muttered to themselves, some made slight gestures, as if anticipating the conversation in which they would shortly be engaged, some wore the cunning look of bargaining and plotting, some were anxious and eager, some slow and dull; in some countenances, were written gain; in others, loss."

They find shelter for the night by a blast furnace, which to their eyes looks like a vision of hell, with the beating of hammers and the roar of furnaces, and the workers moving like demons among the flames and smoke. But almost more frightening is the blighted country that lies outside the city. First "a long suburb of red brick houses – some with patches of garden-ground, where coal-dust and factory smoke darkened the shrinking leaves, and coarse rank flowers, and where the struggling vegetation sickened and sank under the hot breath of kiln and furnace, making them by its presence seem yet more blighting and unwholesome than in the town itself." And then they enter a region where not a blade of grass can grow, where the only green that can live is the cloud on the surface of stagnant pools.

"On every side, and far as the eye could see into the heavy distance, tall chimneys, crowding on each other, and presenting that endless repetition of the same dull, ugly, form, which is the horror of oppressive dreams, poured out their plague of smoke, obscured the light, and made foul the melancholy air. On mounds of ashes by the wayside, sheltered only by a few rough penthouse roofs, strange engines spun and writhed like tortured creatures; clanking their iron chains, shrieking in their rapid whirl from time to time as though in torment unendurable, and making the ground tremble with their agonies.

"Dismantled houses here and there appeared, tottering to the earth, propped up by fragments of others that had fallen down, unroofed, window-less, blackened, desolate, but yet inhabited. Men, women, children, wan in their looks and ragged in attire, tended the engines, fed their tributary fire, begged upon the road, or scowled half-naked from the doorless houses."

Nell begs at one of the wretched hovels for a morsel of bread for her grand-father. "'Do you see that?' returned the man hoarsely, pointing to a kind of bundle on the ground. 'That's a dead child. I and five hundred other men were thrown out of work, three months ago. That is my third dead child, and last. Do you think *I* have charity to bestow, or a morsel of bread to spare?'"

It was then with this hideous poverty, with this tangled, uncontrolled sprawl of industry that the Victorians found themselves, and with an urban civilization growing so rapidly that it seemed to threaten their whole way of life. They were the pioneers; the new factory age reached England first, and they had to work out some cure to the evils which resulted from it.

The writers of the time, wholly unused to the idea of industry organized in factories instead of in small scattered groups, regarded it with horror as something wholly unnatural, something which turned human beings into slaves. "Whilst the engine runs, the people must work – men, women, and children yoked together with iron and steam. The animal machine . . . is chained fast to the iron machine, which knows no suffering and no weariness," wrote Sir James Kay-Shuttleworth in 1832. Taine in the 1860's looked on the Manchester mills as something monstrous and soul-destroying, "a Babel built of brick," he called the city, and the factories seemed to him like colossal prisons, where thousands of men were penned, engaged in unnatural labour.

AT WORK IN A BREWERY – MIXING THE MALT
To Doré this scene took on the aspect of an inferno. (*London, 1872.*)

Dickens wrote in a similar vein in his description of Coketown in *Hard Times*, where the machine dominates the lives of the workers, and the latter are reduced to faceless anonymity.

"It was a town of machinery and tall chimneys, out of which interminable serpents of smoke trailed themselves for ever and ever, and never got uncoiled. It had a black canal in it, and a river that ran purple with ill-smelling dye, and vast piles of building full of windows where there was a rattling and a trembling all day long, and where the piston of the steam-engine worked monotonously up and down, like the head of an elephant in a state of melancholy madness. It contained several large streets all very like one another, and many small streets still more like one another, inhabited by people equally like one another, who all went in and out at the same hours, with the same sound upon the same pavements, to do the same work, and to whom every day was the same as yesterday and to-morrow, and every year the counterpart of the last and the next."

Dickens used this image of the melancholy mad elephant throughout *Hard Times* to symbolize the remorseless monster of industry, that never tired, and drove its wretched slaves before it.

But the fact was that the lot of the unskilled labourer had never been a pleasant one, particularly since the Napoleonic Wars had cast their blight upon agribulture in England. It was no new thing for women and children to labour long hours at wholly unsuitable work and in miserable conditions, or for families to live in the foulest squalor. The new element was the machine, and the concentration of many thousands of workers within one building during the day, and in grossly over-populated city slums during their leisure. It was this concentration of population, this subjection to the machine, that outraged Dickens and Taine, who had probably never been aware of the wretched gangs of women and children in the country, marshalled under gang-leaders to labour in the fields; the men who might have to walk four or five miles to their work, spend all day in wet clothes, walk back again in the dark, with no prospect of anything ahead of them but the workhouse when they grew too infirm to struggle any longer.

Not all factory labour, by any means, offered worse conditions than the agricultural labourer's. But what was worse even than the labourer's tumbledown cottage with its clay floor and hole in the thatch were the conditions in which the town worker lived before reformers and planners had come to grips with the new industrial cities which had sprung up so rapidly since the 1780's. As G. M. Young wrote sombrely: "The imagination can hardly apprehend the horror in which thousands of families [130] years ago were born, dragged out their ghastly lives, and died: drinking water brown with faecal particles, the corpses kept unburied for a fortnight in a festering London August; mortified limbs quivering with maggots; courts where not a weed would grow, and sleeping-dens afloat with sewage."

The factory worker, too, had become anonymous, swallowed up in streets where nobody knew him and nobody cared what happened to him. In the country the labourer would have been part of a small community, known to the people about him, with the squire and the clergyman to keep an eye upon him. Such concern as there was for the welfare of the working man was exercised by the landowner and the clergy, and once the town had swallowed him up he was beyond their reach. The Church, like everything else in those early days of the industrial age, had no resources to deal with the huge new city population; not only were churches and clergy lacking to serve them, there was not even a sufficiency of graveyards in which to bury them. And the attitude of the factory owner towards the

BRITISH INDIFFERENCE TO THE HORRORS OF CITY LIFE
Britannia sleeps on surrounded by scenes of death and desolation, oblivious to the miseries of the city poor and the threats to the health of the population. *Punch,* 1849.

hands he employed was rarely the paternal one of the squire towards those who lived on his land. Even the conscientious employer could not be expected to affect the lives of his workers in the way that a landowner whose family had lived on the same estate among the same people for generations was able to do.

There were those who tried to carry the paternal tradition into industry. Sir Titus Salt, for instance, built his works in the open country, surrounding the mill with houses for his workers, and providing, besides some 800 dwellings, a school, a church, a park, and an institute. 'Charity', that the country cottager so often fiercely resented, had no place at Saltaire; everything had to be paid for, even though the sum demanded might be very small. Alcohol was not allowed in Saltaire, and the words "All beer abandon ye that enter here" greeted those approaching this industrial community. The Cadburys at Bourneville and the Levers at Port Sunlight later in the century founded industrial communities on the Salt pattern.

Disraeli in *Sybil* described such a Utopia. The benevolent millowner, Mr. Trafford, lives among his workpeople in a garden city that surrounds the mill. Disraeli believed strongly in the influence for good of the fatherly squire, and thought that an extension of this into industrial life was the best possible way of ensuring the health, happiness, and good morals of the worker. "Proximity to the employer brings cleanliness and order, because it brings observation and encouragement. In the settlement of Trafford crime was positively unknown, and offences were very slight."

In stark contrast to Trafford, with its orderly behaviour and benevolent despotism on the part of the ruling family, is the district of Wodgate which Disraeli describes in the same novel. Here there is anarchy, every man fighting for himself in a community which began by being a settlement of squatters on land that belonged to nobody, and developed in the course of 25 years into a sprawl of industry, where the masters labour in their own houses, surrounded by their apprentices, on whom they inflict the most hideous cruelties, but who, according to Disraeli, labour on supported by the belief that their day to be masters and oppressors will surely arrive. Wodgate possesses no church, there is no sort of municipal government, no schools, no public services, "nor does any one know anything except his business." Wodgate was taken from an actual district in the neighbour-hood of Birmingham.

Sybil did not excite attention so much for Disraeli's descriptions of industrial conditions as for his denunciation of the "two nations" into which England, he said, was divided, and which provided the sub-title for the novel.

"'Two nations: between whom there is no intercourse and no sympathy; who are as ignorant of each other's habits, thoughts, and feelings, as if they were dwellers in different zones, or inhabitants of different planets; who are formed by a different breeding, are fed by a different food, are ordered by different manners, and are not governed by the same laws.'

'You speak of—' said Egremont, hesitatingly.

'THE RICH AND THE POOR.'"

The image of the two nations seized the public imagination, and constant reference was made to it by those interested in the problems of the poor of the industrial age.

Much of the writing of the middle decades of the century reflects this interest. Douglas Jerrold, who enjoyed a great reputation at the time as a wit and a humorous writer, complained in explanation of the failure of his plays, that in 1833 no one was thinking about the poor, and in 1839 nobody was thinking about anything else. Novelists used the material to be found in the official reports of the 30's and 40's on the working and living conditions of the industrial poor. There is, for example, Mrs. Frances Trollope's *The Life and Adventure of Michael Armstrong the Factory Boy.* Published in 1840, at a time when the Factory Act of 1833 had put an end to the worst exploitation of child labour in textile factories, it set down in fearful detail the lives that children might have led in the worst mills in the pre-1833 period. We see a vicious and sadistic mill owner, children with crippled, distorted limbs, maimed by exposure to dangerous machinery and by brutal attacks from the factory overseer, dragged to work fainting with weariness by desperate mothers, or scrambling to steal food from the pigs' troughs.

Better books, and based upon observation rather than on a mere reading of sensational exposures of factory cruelties, are Mrs. Gaskell's novels of Manchester and its workers: *Mary Barton* (1848) and *North and South* (1854–5). She was married to the minister of a Unitarian chapel in Manchester, and saw for herself the miseries that the trade depression brought to Manchester, the lack of understanding that existed between the mill-owners and their workers, the despair of men who saw their jobs being given to imported cheap Irish labour, the suffering of their starving families, and how ordinary, decent men could be turned into Chartists and assassins and mob-leaders.

Mary Barton describes the Manchester that we find in Engels' *Condition of the Working Class*, where the poor die of fever in wet and filthy cellars. The iron enters John Barton's soul when, with the knowledge that his small son is dying of starvation, he watches his employer's wife come out of a grocer's shop and step into her carriage, laden with delicacies for a party. This is what gives a man a hatred for the class that employs him.

There were some who accused Mrs. Gaskell of treating the mill-owners too harshly in *Mary Barton*. In *North and South* she made a mill-owner one of her central characters and presented his point of view as well as his employees'. This is Manchester at the time of the trade depression when businesses are crashing, wages cut, and starving men, frantic with despair

A MOTHER DRAGGING AN EXHAUSTED CHILD-WORKER
TO THE MILL

Illustration from *Michael Armstrong, the Factory Boy,* 1840.

as they see their children crying for food, are striking for more money. John Thornton the mill-owner is a self-made Lancashire man who has pulled himself up to his present position by implacable persistence and self-denial, and cannot see why it is not open for any one of his mill-hands to do the same. To the clergyman's daughter from the south, who is appalled by his apparent harshness, and the dry merciless way in which he reduces the factory system to axioms of trade, instead of seeing it as she would wish, in terms of flesh and blood, he tries to explain his attitude and those of his brother manufacturers. His theory is that his interests are the same as those of his workpeople, and they must both rise or sink together according to the state of trade. He will use his discretion to make good decisions "'but I will neither be forced to give my reasons, nor flinch from what I have once declared to be my resolution. Let them turn out! I shall suffer as well as they: but at the end they will find I have not bated nor altered one jot.'"

Proud and independent himself, he recognizes that his hands have a right to be proud and independent too, and the idea of any interference with their lives after working hours disgusts him. He reckons to be absolute master of them while they are on his premises, and they are their own masters at the end of the day. Mrs. Gaskell has given a very fair account of the new relationship between master and employee that the industrial age brought about, in contrast to the feudal dependence upon the landowner that existed in agricultural life. To this new relationship both master and man had to adjust themselves.

Dickens in *Dombey and Son* (1847–8) presented another aspect of the industrial age, the railways, which were blasting their way into the towns in the 1840's, altering their physical appearance and bringing a new sort of life, destroying the isolation in which the remoter parts of England had lived, and bringing the different classes into closer contact. Dickens described the effect that railway building had upon one London district:

"The first shock of a great earthquake had, just at that period, rent the whole neighbourhood to its centre. Traces of its course were visible on every side. Houses were knocked down; streets broken through and stopped; deep pits and trenches dug in the ground; enormous heaps of earth and clay thrown up; buildings were undermined and shaking, propped by great beams of wood. Here, a chaos of carts, overthrown and jumbled together, lay topsy-turvy at the bottom of a steep unnatural hill; there, confused

BUILDING RAILWAYS ACROSS LONDON
Digging new graves in St. Pancras churchyard, to replace those disturbed by the
railway track, 1866.
Navvies at work on the Midland railway at King's Cross, 1867.

treasures of iron soaked and rusted in something that had accidentally become a pond. Everywhere were bridges that led nowhere; thoroughfares that were wholly impassable; Babel towers of chimneys, wanting half their height; temporary wooden houses and enclosures, in the most unlikely situations; carcasses of ragged tenements, and fragments of unfinished walls and arches, and piles of scaffolding, and wildernesses of bricks, and giant forms of cranes, and tripods straddling above nothing. . . .

"In short, the yet unfinished and opened Railroad was in progress; and, from the very core of this dire disorder, trailed smoothly away, upon its mighty course of civilization and destruction."

The inhabitants of this area that is being devoured by the railway watch bewildered, but cannot grasp what is happening. It is an area of "frowsy fields, and cow-houses, and dunghills, and dustheaps, and ditches, and gardens, and summerhouses, and carpet-beating grounds," which is with the coming of the railway being sucked into the great sprawling mass of London. Staggs's Gardens, a dilapidated little row of houses, is sceptical. Its population regards the spot as a sacred grove not to be withered by rail-roads, and is certain that the place will long outlive such ridiculous inven-tions. But the next time we see the spot, some six years later, Staggs's Gardens has been obliterated. The sour no-man's land, not yet town but not country, has been swallowed up by the ever-growing city.

In *Dombey and Son* Dickens presents the railway age, the age of great change. Those who looked on felt it was a new era, that had broken com-pletely with the past. Thackeray, writing the *Roundabout Papers* for the Corn-hill Magazine in the early 1860's when he himself was fifty or so must have voiced the feeling of many of his contemporaries when he said that it was the railroad that divided the old world from the new: "We elderly people have lived in that pre-railroad world, which has passed into limbo and vanished from under us. I tell you it was firm under our feet once, and not long ago. They have raised those railroad embankments up and shut off the old world that was behind them. Climb up that bank on which irons are laid, and look to the other side—it is gone. There *is* no other side..."

In the cities the railways ploughed their way through streets of houses which vanished before them in the way Dickens described in *Dombey*. Much slum property was cleared in this way, and shops, factories, warehouses and offices took its place. But the wretched poor who were displaced fled only to worse slums.

> "Who builds? Who builds? Alas, ye poor!
> If London day by day 'improves',
> Where shall ye find a friendly door
> When every day a home removes?"

lamented a writer in *The Builder* in 1851.

Legislation to improve the lot of the poor of the industrial age, to protect his interests at work and to bring some order and decency into his living conditions abounded throughout Victoria's reign. But the legislation was piecemeal and fragmentary, and in any case very difficult to enforce, for the simple reason that when Parliament passed laws stipulating, for instance, that machinery should be fenced, and limiting the hours that children might work, they could not ensure that there were sufficient inspectors to see that the laws were carried out. And with that peculiar brand of hypocrisy which is a characteristic of the English, there had always been plenty to answer Shaftesbury's denunciations of the fearful conditions in which women and young children were working, with equally passionate cries (which they no doubt believed themselves), that it was in the interest of the British working man that his wife and child should work an 80 hour week, that the country's economy would collapse if they did not – and then where would the workers be? Besides, they said, the children liked it, why would they work so nimbly if they did not?

In *Hard Times* Dickens bitingly satirized this attitude. The Coketown manufacturers had bitterly opposed all attempts to improve the lot of the workers:

"The wonder was [Coketown] was there at all, it had been ruined so often, that it was amazing it had borne so many shocks. Surely there never was such fragile china-ware as that of which the millers of Coketown were made. Handle them never so lightly, and they fell to pieces with such ease that you might suspect them of having been flawed before. They were ruined, when they were required to send labouring children to school; they were ruined when inspectors were appointed to look into their works; they were ruined when such inspectors considered it doubtful whether they were quite justified in chopping people up with their machinery; they were utterly undone, when it was hinted that perhaps they need not always make quite so much smoke ... Another prevalent fiction was very popular there. It took the form of a threat. Whenever a Coketowner felt he was ill-used – that is to say, whenever he was not left entirely alone, and it was proposed to hold him accountable for the consequence of any of his acts – he was sure to come out with the awful menace, that he would 'sooner pitch his property into the Atlantic.' This had terrified the Home Secretary within an inch of his life, on several occasions.

"However, the Coketowners were so patriotic after all, that they never had pitched their property into the Atlantic yet, but, on the contrary, had been kind enough to take mighty good care of it. So there it was, in the haze yonder, and it increased and multiplied."

Fettered with this sort of resistance the reformers moved slowly, eliminating the worst abuses gradually, never able to sweep aside many at any one

in factories, applied at first only to children in cotton mills, was later extended to all children in textile factories, and later still to women as well. But even in the 1860's in the Potteries children often started work at the age of six or seven. An eleven hour day was the best they could hope for, and they were frequently required to work on till late at night in temperatures ranging from 100 to 120 degrees, from which they might well be sent running out on errands on winter nights without stockings, shoes or jackets. Not until 1870 was it laid down that no child under ten years old could be employed, and nobody under thirteen employed full time without an educational certificate.

Similarly, attempts to legislate for the improvement of living conditions in the cities were constantly defeated by the opposition of private interests. It took decades, for instance, for the mounds of human and animal manure to be removed from the streets of the poorer quarters, although there had been no lack of laws made concerning this menace to public health. The fact was that the sale of such manure was very profitable to the landlords, and when the law cut against private interests it was easy to ignore it. Nor was there at the beginning of the Victorian period any adequate municipal government to take charge of the new cities.

Above all the spirit of the English was against interference by the state. They saw fall with dismay bastion after bastion of what they had regarded

"THE CITY NARCISSUS, OR, THE ALDERMAN ENAMOURED
OF HIS DIRTY APPEARANCE"

In this cartoon of 1849 *Punch* attacked the selfish complacency of private individuals who resisted attempts to clear up the filth and squalor of the early
Victorian city.

as their unassailable liberty – liberty to live as they liked, conduct their
works, bring up their children, and keep their houses as they liked. In
outraged fury some high-minded people formed a Private Enterprise
Society in 1849 to oppose the Public Health Act of 1848, which sought
among other things to regulate the supplies of water, the management of
slaughter-houses, and the management of cemeteries.

It was not until comparatively late in the century that there began to be
serious national efforts to fight the problems of the new cities, rather than
local and voluntary efforts. It was only then that it was generally conceded
that the problems must be fought with new weapons, with powers of
"doing away with that form of liberty to which most communities cling,
the sacred power to poison to death not only themselves but their
neighbours."

Reformers throughout the Victorian period found that the best argument
for sanitary reform was that it would actually save money in the long run,

not squander it. But though the ratepayers might accept this in theory they were not so ready to do so in practice; they had to be convinced first that the sums were correct, and second, that the long run was worth bothering about. The idea that the state had an obligation to ensure decent living conditions for everybody, and that landlords had a moral duty to provide it was confined to a few high-minded people like Chadwick[1] and Charles Kingsley and their friends. Most of their contemporaries would feel no shame in considering first what would be the loss or gain to the *landlord* in putting proper drainage into housing for the poor, and it often needed an outbreak of cholera to frighten people into taking action.

Of the Victorian novelists who introduced the theme of sanitary reform into their novels – and it was a frequent topic in the middle years of the century; even Charlotte Yonge, who was usually concerned with more spiritual matters, brought it into *The Three Brides* – Charles Kingsley is by far the most vehement. The heroine of *Yeast* (published in 1848, six years after Chadwick's report) dies in an outbreak of typhus which flares up in the village because of the filthy open drain that runs in front of the cottage. In *Two Years Ago* (1857) the epidemic is cholera, the scene Cornwall. The new doctor has prophesied the outbreak, and urged measures to clean up the drains, but is opposed by the ignorance, pride and laziness of the villagers. The landlord with whom he pleads says that he is being ruined by Free Trade, and cannot afford such luxuries as cleaning out people's drains for them. When the doctor approaches his own senior partner, the old man tells him wrathfully: "'And what be you thinking of, sir, to expect me to offend all my best patients? And not one of 'em but rents some two cottages, some a dozen. And what'll they say to me if I go a routing and rookling in their drains, like an old sow by the wayside, beside putting 'em to all manner of expense? And all on the chance of this cholera coming, which I have no faith in, nor in this new-fangled sanitary reform neither, which is all a dodge for a lot of young Government puppies to fill their pockets, and rule and ride over us; and my opinion always was with the Bible, that 'tis jidgement, sir, a jidgement of God, and we can't escape His holy will, and that's the plain truth of it.'"

This combination of private interest, apathy, and vague belief that epidemics were the will of God was in real life to bedevil the efforts of reformers

1 Sir Edwin Chadwick (1800–90). Public health reformer. Led the enquiry into the Sanitary Conditions of the Working Classes which published its report in 1842.

A LONDON ROOKERY

Devil's Acre, behind the Houses of Parliament, Westminster. This area was once
described as "the moral plague spot of the whole kingdom". Engraving by Doré
(*London,* 1872).

for years to come. But by the second half of the century things were beginning to improve. Sir James Kay-Shuttleworth[1] could report in 1861 that
in Manchester extensive sewering had been undertaken, streets paved,

1 Sir James Phillips Kay-Shuttleworth (1804–77). Secretary to the Manchester Board
of Health, published reports on Manchester working class life. Helped formulate a system
of national education.

flagged, and drained, the 352 streets named as being foul with refuse and stagnant pools had now almost disappeared, pigs had been driven out of houses, smoke from factories reduced, a proper water supply introduced. And some provision had been made for the leisure of the city-dweller – a public library had been founded, parks created, public baths built. Manchester was in fact taking on the aspect which we know now; solid, massive, – and Victorian; a monument to the solidity and respectability of the middle classes who built it.

Each of the great English cities presented its own problems of course, and each developed at its own pace and in its own way. But by the mid-Victorian period, although slums had by no means disappeared, it was generally recognized that they were a social evil to be swept away as soon as possible. To the end of the century great tracts of ancient slums existed in London, the habitual haunt of criminals, very often only a few streets away from the dignified residential squares of the rich in Belgravia and Mayfair. Here, herded together in tall tottering houses built round squalid, filthy courts lived colonies of thieves, vagabonds and beggars, of the sort that Arthur Morrison[1] described in *A Child of The Jago*. Known as rookeries, they had originally been perhaps the site of a sanctuary or a refuge for felons and debtors, or else of some forgotten hospital for the reception of outcasts. They kept this character to the end, and as long as they remained standing were a menacing source of crime and disease. They attracted much attention from writers. Dickens as a child ventured with fascinated horror into the famous Seven Dials rookery, and as an adult inveighed against its horrors. In *Oliver Twist* he described with careful accuracy the Saffron Hill rookery, near Smithfield market.

What struck the observer, novelist or philanthropist, journalist or clergyman, with great force, and what these sought to express in their novels, pamphlets and tracts, were the extremes of affluent living and of destitution that existed in the Victorian city. In London the wealthy lived in the stately squares that stretched in their calm stuccoed dignity north and south of Oxford street – Portman Square, Manchester Square, Grosvenor Square. Or further south, in Belgravia. From there they could drive in the pleasant tree-lined expanses of Hyde Park, ride in Rotten Row or the Ladies' Mile, do a little desultory shopping in the luxurious establishments that lined

1 Arthur Morrison (1863–1945). Novelist, dramatist, authority on Far Eastern art. *A Child of the Jago*, an account of life in London's worst slum, is his best-known work.

STREET MUSICIANS IN A FASHIONABLE LONDON SQUARE, 1846
"Musical beggars" thronged the streets of Victorian cities. *The Illustrated London News,* in a facetious footnote, wondered how many suicides had been brought about by the playing of this particular organ.

Regent street, and the men could walk to their clubs in the St. James's area. On Sundays the family would attend the church that stood, as likely as not, within their own square, where their eyes would fall only upon worshippers of their own social rank.

Around these fashionable districts of west and south-west London were belts of slums, where thousands crouched in fearful poverty. But of these thousands the carefree resident of Eaton Square or Bryanston Square could, if he chose, remain oblivious. There were beggars, of course, who obtruded themselves, but the servants could keep these away from your house, and in the streets you were riding in your own carriage and you could turn away your head.

Of this sort of wilful blindness we get an instance in a children's book of 1879, *Victoria Bess* by 'Brenda', where the only daughter of wealthy, adoring parents drives with her cherished new doll (who is dressed in a feathered bonnet and a velvet pelisse trimmed with swansdown) to Richmond to buy some cakes, and is outraged because two "dirty little street girls" gaze through the carriage window in admiration at the doll. Dickens was savage about this sort of selfish blindness. "Look round upon the world of odious sights – millions of immortal creatures have no other world on earth – at the lightest mention of which humanity revolts, and dainty delicacy living in the next street, stops her ears, and lisps 'I don't believe it!'"

9 · *Life in Mean Streets*

THE novelist George Gissing who described the life of the poor in the last decades of the Victorian age, called it the nether world; that lower, sub-merged world out of which, he insisted, it was impossible to raise oneself.

It was a world that he knew well, one from which, in his own mind, he was always struggling to extricate himself, always afraid of sinking back into its mire. But there were within it, even among those down-trodden millions who thronged the mean streets of Victorian cities, a multitude of social classes – who looked down upon each other, and felt a great deal of satisfaction that they were a rung higher in the ladder than the set below them. Gissing in his novel *The Nether World* (1889) said that the great divide came between those who did and those who did not wear a collar; between, in effect, the skilled and the unskilled worker. Each of these classes, he admitted, could be endlessly sub-divided. What a gap there was, for instance, between the mechanic with his collar attached to a flannel shirt and just visible along the top of a black tie, and the shopman who proudly modelled his collars on the styles affected by the aristocracy. And among those who wore a neckcloth instead of a collar, one might discriminate in the same way. The navvy, the scaffolder, the costermonger, the cab-tout

A lavender seller. Engraving by Doré.

– all of them would indicate by the way they folded or knotted their neck attire the social difference of which they themselves were acutely aware, though others might not be.

The Nether World describes some of these descending orders of misery in what, to Gissing's mind, was a world without hope, without prospect of relief. The scene is the Clerkenwell area of London in the 1880's, an area of factories and workrooms and small industries, where men, says Gissing, work through the livelong day, through all the years of life that are granted them, straining their eyesight, overtaxing their muscles, "without prospect or hope of reward save the permission to eat and sleep and bring into the world other creatures to strive with them for bread."

At the bottom of this abyss of misery, hardly better than the destitute described in chapter ten, is the Candy family, who crouch in a room in a filthy slum, unfurnished, sleeping on rags. The father is a journeyman baker, working nineteen hours a day, the son a potman at a public-house, working from eight until midnight. The mother is a habitual drunkard, who drinks away any money that comes into her hands, the daughter scrapes together a few pence stitching shirts – a needle slave, Gissing calls her. When the father deserts the mother, maddened by her persistent drinking, the son contrives to pay the rent somehow, and scrounge a little food and a few pennyworth of coal. "It was very seldom indeed that the Candys had more of anything in their room than would last them for the current day." And there is no time nor energy to spare for human feelings, nor for a kind word.

In a higher grade of misery are the Hewetts. They live in two rooms in lodgings, not in squalor, but in what Gissing calls "the chill discomfort of poverty." John Hewett is a skilled carpenter, now out of work and trudging the streets to find some sort of employment, however mean, that will pay the rent and feed his family. Things had once been better with him; a new baby had been a source of joy, not an additional burden; there had been good food in the house, he had been able to be a little particular about where he sent his eldest child to school. State education for all had been provided since 1870, but "a prejudice then (and still) common among workpeople of decent habits made him hesitate about sending his girl to sit side by side with the children of the streets." So he sent her to a Church school where he would have had to make a contribution to the fees.

When Gissing introduces us to this family things have changed very

A SLUM COURT
Orange Court, Drury Lane.
Engraving by Doré (*London,* 1872).

much for the worse, but the Hewetts still live in far greater decency than the Candys. There are a few pictures on the walls, some ornaments on the mantelpiece, furniture in the rooms. The family is undernourished and wretched, but there is still affection among them, and the children come forward to be greeted when their father returns; poverty has not driven all feelings of humanity from them as it has with Mrs. Candy. So when the eldest Hewett boy wants to marry Pennyloaf Candy (her real name is Penelope), the Hewetts feel that he is lowering himself.

The Peckovers in their turn despise the Hewetts. Mrs. Peckover owns the lodgings where the Hewetts live. She is a widow with a handsome bit of capital behind her, gained by selling a beer-shop which she used to run. Clem Peckover is employed in an artificial flower-factory, and what she earns more than covers her keep. The Peckovers keep a wretched little servant girl whom they half-starve and treat as a slave. With some leisure and money to spare, life is not just grinding anxiety.

At the top of the 'nether world' are the Byasses. He is a clerk in a whole-sale stationers, and he comes therefore into Gissing's collared category, and wears a brown silk hat into the bargain. Socially speaking, there is little between him and Mr. Pooter; they both belong to the lower middle class rather than to the working class. The Byasses live in their own house, in a road where there are dwelling houses only – no mean shops, pawn-brokers, or public-houses. They have the energy and spirits to be gay and affectionate towards each other, a thing undreamt of by the Candys. They can cherish their baby. To such as the Candys a new baby is an anxiety, the death of one a cause of dull relief.

The details that Gissing gives of the meals eaten by these four families affords a further insight into their way of living. Pennyloaf Candy pawns a petticoat and a skirt for eighteenpence, and buys a pennyworth of coal (this buys seven pounds) which she carries back in her apron; enough to boil water for tea of which she has also bought a pennyworth, together with a ha'p'orth of milk.

When John Hewett comes home from tramping the streets in search of work, his wife gives him "a scrap of cold steak, left over from yesterday, and still upon the original dish amid congealed fat; a spongy half-quartern loaf... a shapeless piece of something purchased under the name of butter, dabbed into a shallow basin; some pickled cabbage in a tea-cup; and, lastly, a pot of tea, made by adding a teaspoonful or two to the saturated leaves which had already served at breakfast and mid-day. This repast was laid on a very dirty cloth. The cups were unmatched and chipped, the knives were in all stages of decreptitude; the teapot was of dirty tin, with a damaged spout."

Clem Peckover settles down with vast enjoyment to a supper of five sausages (blackened, because she has several times caught the pan on fire during their cooking), which she eats with a great quantity of bread and washes down with beer. Gissing describes the girl's brutish manner of consuming this meal with a disgust that suggests that he had often to witness such a sight.

The Byasses, on the other hand, eat comfortably and well, and are able to welcome a guest to a meal. "Supper was soon ready in the comfortable kitchen. A cold shoulder of mutton, a piece of cheese, pickled beetroot, a seed-cake, and raspberry jam; such was the fare to which Bessie Byass invited her husband and guest."

Other writers confirm Gissing's account of the lives of the poor. The

"MAMMON'S RENTS"

Punch published this drawing in 1883 to draw attention to conditions described in *The Bitter Cry of Outcast London.*

Rev. Andrew Mearns, for instance, a few years before in his *Bitter Cry of Outcast London* had described conditions just such as the Candys lived in. Many novelists wrote about the plight of the hopelessly poor classes; Gissing differed from these only in his profound gloom. He could not use their sufferings to urge a campaign of reform; to inspire or uplift in the style of the tract writers. He had lived among them, he had married from them (one wife turned out an alcoholic, the other bad-tempered to the point of insanity); he could only feel hopeless despair when he contemplated them. Mrs. Gaskell could describe in *Mary Barton* and *North and South* instances of how the nobility of the human soul had triumphed over fearful surroundings; Dickens used their situation to rouse tears and compassion, or he could write amusingly about their social distinctions and gentilities. Gissing saw the poor as Taine had seen them:

"Numerous are the faces among workmen and day labourers in the country which are deeply lined, very pale, worn out by fatigue, making one think of those old cab-horses one sees standing patient and inert, their legs splayed, while the rain pours down their lean old flanks. Lank, greying hair, rather sparse, the mouth hanging half-open as if the muscles had given way of their own accord; the eyes have an almost sightless look of indifference. The man is still functioning, but it seems as if this must be due simply to momentum: he has become a machine."

The earnings of men such as these were pitiful even if they were fully employed, and many of them could find no work. Others were self-employed, they toiled at such tasks as pasting up matchboxes – in the room that also housed them and their family. Mearns refers to the unhealthy occupations followed by many of the slum-dwellers. "Here you are choked as you enter by the air laden with particles of the superfluous fur pulled from the skins of rabbits, rats, and dogs and other animals in their preparation for the furrier. Here the smell of paste and of drying match-boxes, mingling with other sickly odours, overpowers you; or it may be the fragrance of stale fish or vegetables, not sold on the day previously, and kept in the room overnight."

A child, he said, could make 10s. 6d. a week by thieving. Who could blame him if he preferred to do this than stick matchboxes, for which twopence farthing a gross was given. Women who stitched trousers received twopence ha'penny a pair. A woman might make a shilling a day this way. "But what does a day mean to this poor soul? *Seventeen hours*! From five in the morning to ten at night – no pause for meals. She eats her crust and drinks a little tea as she works, making in very truth, not her living only but her shroud." It was, however, one of the few occupations open to a woman with children, and though it might ruin her eyesight and destroy her health, she was forced to persist – or see her children go hungry. Others might mind a few children for mothers who were out at work, or, if they possessed a mangle, take in their neighbours' washing.

In conditions such as these, drink was the only escape. For a penny or two you could get enough gin to make you forget for a couple of hours the drudgery and hopelessness of your life, the children crying for food, the rent-collector beating on the door of the den where you lived. Mearns estimated that round his chapel near Leicester Square there was one public-house to every hundred people, counting men, women, and children. "Look into one of these glittering saloons, with its motley, miserable crowd, and you may be horrified as you think of the evil that is nightly wrought there; but contrast it with any of the abodes which you find in the fetid courts behind them, and you will wonder no longer that it is crowded. With its brightness, its excitement, and its temporary forget-fulness of misery, it is a comparative haven to tens of thousands. How can they be expected to resist its temptations? They could not live if they did not drink, even though they know that by drinking they do worse than die."

Drink dulled ravenous hunger, gave temporary warmth. The streets of the Victorian cities held many shivering wretches who begged from passers-by a couple of pence to buy them a glass of gin. Hawthorne, com-menting with horror on the Liverpool poor, said that at every ten steps or so there were Spirit Vaults. Taine too was appalled at what he saw for himself and at what he was told. He prefaced his figures for the high inci-dence of drunkeness among the English and the amount of alcohol sold (in 1848 there were 11,000 spirit shops in London as against 4,000 butchers and bakers) with a remark about his missing laundry. He had enquired about this, and had been told by the laundry proprietor that there had been a public holiday that week and all the laundresses therefore were drunk.

The Victorian philanthropists, and the responsible members of the

THE GIN SHOP
Illustration by Cruickshank to Dickens' *Sketches by Boz.*

community were fully aware of the enormous gravity of this problem. Many were the Temperance Societies, and innumerable the little booklets and stories that pointed out the dangers of drink and urged total abstinence. Taine spoke of the posters of one of these societies which showed a drunkard lying stupefied while imps removed his heart and brain in shovelfuls, the principal devil standing by with a bottle of gin. The punning slogan was "My Best Spirit." Tremendous energy went into efforts to persuade the Victorian working man and woman "to take the pledge" and renounce drinking. Many of the poor saw the dangers and signed the pledge. But whether they would have the strength of will to keep it was another matter. In *The Nether World* there is a pitiful account of Mrs. Candy who, in the last stages of disease induced by drink, with everything sold to buy it, still has pinned on her walls five pledges of total abstinence, representing five separate attempts to give up the habit, signed in handwriting that grows progressively more wavering. This becomes even more pitiful when it is known that Gissing's first wife, whom he finally abandoned because of her alcoholism, was found dead in a room decorated in the same way.

Dickens commented on the English vice of heavy drinking, and the well-meaning efforts to cure it, in *Sketches by Boz*.

"Well-disposed gentlemen, and charitable ladies, would alike turn with coldness and disgust from a description of the drunken besotted men, and wretched broken down miserable women, who form no inconsiderable portion of the frequenters of these [gin-shops]; forgetting, in the pleasant consciousness of their own rectitude, the poverty of the one, and the temptation of the other. Gin-drinking is a great vice in England, but wretchedness and dirt are a greater; and until you improve the homes of the poor, or persuade a half-famished wretch not to seek relief in the temporary oblivion of his own misery, with the pittance which, divided among his family, would furnish a morsel of bread for each, gin-shops will increase in number and splendour. If Temperance Societies would suggest an antidote against hunger, filth, and foul air, or could establish dispensaries for the gratuitous distribution of Lethe-water, gin-palaces would be numbered among the things that were."

For a brief period the lives of these wretched people might be carefree – when they were young, earning a bit of money, and still unmarried. Holidays were few, but Sundays, and such occasions as the August Bank Holiday, were the time for rowdy high spirits, associated with much heavy drinking. Gissing describes in *The Nether World* the August Bank Holiday which serves Pennyloaf Candy for her honeymoon. "Throw wide the doors of the temple of Alcohol!" comments Gissing bitterly. "Behold we come in our thousands, jingling the coins that shall purchase us this one day of tragical mirth." For Pennyloaf it is tragical enough. Her husband, to whom she has been married only that morning, takes her on an excursion to the Crystal Palace, in the southern suburbs of London.

THE LONDONER'S BANK HOLIDAY OUTING
A penny ride by paddle steamer down the Thames to Greenwich (*Illustrated London News,* 1847).

He is nineteen, she is sixteen. She has new clothes for the first time in her life, and a gleaming gold ring. "Gold, Pennyloaf, real gold! The pawnbroker would lend her seven-and-sixpence on it, any time." Her husband spends money lavishly on the amusements, on the roundabout, the coconuts, the swings. Then he starts drinking, then quarrelling, then fighting. Pennyloaf returns home with all her new clothes ruined, and the certainty that tomorrow she will have to pawn her ring.

The expectation of life among these, the very poor, was not long. Visiting foreigners commented on their stunted appearance, their flabby flesh, and grey or yellow skin. They died as they lived, huddled in the miserable dens that served them for homes. For doctors they had the sort that Arthur Morrison described in *A Child of the Jago.*

"One of half a dozen such [shops] kept by a medical man who lived away from them, and bothered himself as little about them as was consistent with banking and takings and signing the death-certificates. A needy young student, whose sole qualification was cheapness, was set to do the business of each place, and the uniform price for advice and medicine was sixpence."

For the chronic sick, with no one to tend them, there was the workhouse infirmary, but the following chapter shows something of the horror that this institution held for the poor. There were voluntary hospitals in the big cities, but as likely as not you would need a letter from a subscriber to get admitted, and even should you manage to obtain one, how was the sick person to be conveyed to the hospital? There was, besides, a general fear of such places.

The Victorian poor saved not so much as an insurance against illness, but to cover the cost of their burial, to ensure that they were not buried by the parish as a pauper, a last hideous disgrace that it was worth starvation during one's life to avoid. The money could be hoarded at home, or it could be saved with a Burial Club, a few coppers being deposited each week with a fellow workman. But there were plenty of instances of fraud and dishonesty among the treasurers, or just plain incompetence. Gissing describes the tragedy of a man who discovers at the same time as he realizes his wife is dying, that the secretary of the society with whom he has saved has absconded with the funds.

"To John Hewett the blow was a terrible one. In spite of his poverty, he has never fallen behind with those weekly payments. The thing he dreaded supremely was, that his wife or one of the children should die and he be unable to provide a decent burial. At the death of the last child born to him the club had of course paid, and the confidence he felt in it for the future was a sensible support under the many miseries of his life, a support of which no idea can be formed by one who has never foreseen the possibility of those dear to him being carried to a pauper's grave."

John Hewett, though nearly distracted by need for money was not, as we have seen, in the same category as the Candys, whom he despised as belonging to a class utterly removed from his own. Arthur Morrison, in an introduction to a collection of short stories, *Tales of Mean Streets* (1894), gives some account of the lives of those who pride themselves on being far removed from slum dwellers. These poor live in a street of dingy little brick houses in London, twenty feet high, with three square holes to carry the windows and an oblong hole to carry the door. Turnings from the street lead to less respectable streets, streets where "mangling done here" stares from windows and front doors are left carelessly open and squalid women

EARLY MORNING – THE WORKMAN'S TRAIN·
One of the first underground railways. Engraving by Doré (*London, 1872*).

sit on the doorsteps and girls go to work in the factories. But the dwellers in the street that Arthur Morrison describes stand aloof from those sort of people. Some of them are employed in the docks, some in the gasworks, some as shipbuilders. They live two families in a house (the houses in this street have six rooms apiece), unless lodgers are taken in, or there are grown sons paying for bed and board. The grown daughters marry as soon as they can, and until then are employed mostly in millinery and dressmaking – "respectable" situations. They would consider domestic service as socially beneath them, and factory work lower still.

Every morning the street echoes with the sound of the night watchman or the early policeman knocking up the workers. It costs fourpence a week to be wakened in this way, and the knocking will continue until there is a muffled acknowledgement from within.

"The knocking and the shouting pass, and there comes the noise of opening and shutting of doors, and a clattering away to the docks, the gasworks, and the ship-yards. Later more door-shutting is heard, and then the trotting of sorrow-laden little feet along the grim street to the grim Board School three grim streets off. Then silence, save for a subdued sound of scrubbing here and there, and the puny squall of croupy infants. After this, a new trotting of little feet to docks, gasworks and ship-yards with father's dinner in a basin and a red handkerchief, and to the Board School again. More muffled scrubbing and more squalling, and perhaps a feeble attempt or two at decorating the blankness of a square hole here and there by pouring water into a grimy flower-pot full of dirt. Then comes the trot of little feet towards the oblong holes, heralding the slower tread of sooty artisans; a smell of bloater up and down; nightfall; the fighting of boys in the street, perhaps of men at the corner near the beer-shop; sleep. And this is the record of a day in this street; and every day is hopelessly the same."

Sunday varies the week a little. Children in Sunday boots trot to the bake-house to bring back the family dinner of beef, potatoes and batter pudding that is being cooked there. Some families, the fathers dressed in black suits, the children with polished faces, may go to chapel. But most of the men lie on their beds and read the Sunday paper, or hang around waiting for the beer-shop to open.

Morrison describes a small shop in this street: "Half a dozen candles, a few sickly sugarsticks, certain shrivelled bloaters, some bootlaces, and a bundle or two or firewood compose a stock which at night is sometimes lighted by a little paraffin lamp in a tin sconce, and sometimes by a candle." It is kept by a widow who washes and chars all day, and sews cheap shirts at night. She nurses a hatred for a neighbour who has met her coming out of a pawnshop.

Gissing's Candy family would feel no shame in visiting the pawnshop, but to the more respectable poor it would clearly be anguish and shame. Morrison in *Tales of Mean Streets* includes a story of two women who "keep themselves to themselves", and struggle to support themselves first by keep-ing a little school, then by giving piano lessons at sixpence a lesson. At last they are reduced to selling the piano, and at length to pawning their belongings surreptitiously, one by one, unknown to the hawk-eyed and curious neighbours. One day, when no trace of them has been seen for a week, the landlord breaks into the house. Both women are dead from under-nourishment, in a house from which all the furnishings have vanished, except the curtains and the wax fruit under a glass shade which stands in the parlour window giving genteel respectability to the house.

This world where genteel respectability struggled with acute poverty

THE PAWNBROKER'S SHOP
Illustration by Cruickshank to Dickens' *Sketches by Boz*.

Dickens knew well. His father had been a clerk in the Navy Pay Office with a hopeless inability to live within his income, and Dickens' later childhood was punctuated by a series of removals from one house to another, while his father struggled with feeble ineffectuality to free himself from the morass of debts that threatened to close over the family's heads.

By the time he was eleven the family (John and Elizabeth Dickens, six children, a lodger, and a little maid-of-all-work) were living in a four-roomed house with basement and garret in Camden Town – then a newly .built suburb of London. They had as neighbours a washerwoman and a Bow Street runner, so it was hard for them to hold their heads high. Money difficulties were acute, and creditors were pressing for payment, and Mrs.

Dickens had the idea that a school might put the family finances into better order. So the family moved to a larger house, with a very much larger rent, and fastened a brass plate inscribed MRS. DICKENS'S ESTABLISH-MENT to the front door. Charles and the little maid were sent to distribute leaflets advertising the school. But as Charles Dickens remarked in adult life: "Nobody ever came to the school, nor do I recollect that anybody ever proposed to come, or that the least preparation was made to receive anybody."

The parents began selling or pawning their household goods in a frantic attempt to appease the angry tradesmen who came and bellowed demands for money up the staircase. Charles was often sent on these errands. But worse was to come to him. A friend of the family offered the boy a job in a blacking warehouse at six shillings a week. John Dickens had brought up his son to regard himself as a young gentleman, and to be reduced to sticking labels on to pots of blacking in the company of common boys with un-couth accents and manners was to the young Charles unspeakable degrada-tion.

Eleven days after he began this work his father was arrested for debt. For the first three nights, according to the practice of the times, John Dickens was lodged in the "sponging house" kept by the bailiff while he desperately tried to raise the money. But it was useless; he was taken to the Marshalsea prison, and there his wife and four of the children joined him. It is typical of the family that even in this final humiliation they should try to demon-strate to the little world of the Marshalsea that they were gentlefolk – they took with them the little maid-of-all-work to attend upon them.

"Thirty years ago," wrote Dickens in *Little Dorrit*, "there stood a few doors short of the church of Saint George in the borough of Southwark, on the left-hand side of the way going southward, the Marshalsea Prison. It had stood there many years before, and it remained there some years afterwards; but it is gone now, and the world is none the worse without it.

It was an oblong pile of barrack building, partitioned into squalid houses standing back to back, so that there were no back rooms; environed by a narrow paved yard, hemmed in by high walls duly spiked at top."

Behind these walls for nearly a quarter of a century William Dorrit is imprisoned. Dickens's father was there for only three months before a

THE FLEET DEBTORS' PRISON
This prison was abolished in 1842 and demolished in 1846.
The racket ground.

legacy from his mother enabled him to settle his debt, but Dorrit bears many resemblances to him.

When we meet Dorrit in the opening chapters of the novel he has long ago put behind him his early shame at finding himself in this predicament. He is the senior debtor, the Father of the Marshalsea the others call him, and he rules his little world with pitiful airs and graces. The other inmates accept this, and the custom grows up whereby departing, freed debtors, prisoners no longer, hand over a few silver coins with much deference to the Father of the Marshalsea; tribute money, which he accepts with great dignity. There is a moving moment when a working man, a plasterer, who has been in the Marshalsea for only a week and has now settled his debt, hands his tribute to William Dorrit in the form of a pile of halfpence.

"The Grate", where prisoners begged for
alms from the outside world.

Interior of "the Grate".

"The Father of the Marshalsea had never been offered tribute in copper yet. His children often had, and with his perfect acquiescence it had gone into the common purse, to buy meat that he had eaten, and drink that he had drunk; but fustian splashed with white lime, bestowing halfpence on him, front to front, was new.

'How dare you!' he said to the man, and feebly burst into tears."

Dickens sees perfectly how after a quarter of a century's imprisonment Dorrit's pitiful dignity is all that is left to him. For one agonizing moment this has been stripped from him and he is forced to see himself as he really is, an object of charity to a common working man who is far better off than he is, because the plasterer is a freed man, clear of debt. Dickens's insight into the feelings of that class which is struggling not to be pulled down into the abysses of "the nether world" was never greater than at this moment.

The child Dickens did feel at the time of his father's imprisonment that he had been swallowed up by the nether world. He had seen the family's house in Gower street gradually emptied of its possessions until only a few beds and chairs were left. Then his mother and the younger children had gone to join the father in the Marshalsea, while Charles stayed outside, alone in lodgings, creeping to his hated work in the blacking warehouse every day, wandering round the streets at night, hungry and desperately lonely. A few weeks after his father left the Marshalsea Charles was taken from the warehouse. He had spent at the most only five months there, but the agony was so great that he could never bear to speak about it afterwards; not even his wife or children were told. From his sufferings at this time comes the deep concern of his novels with the sufferings of children at the hands of a harsh, unfeeling adult world.

In *David Copperfield* Dickens made direct use of his own experiences. The young David is sent to work at the age of ten, washing bottles in a City warehouse. He lodges with Mr. Micawber who, like Dickens' father, is forever in debt, and forever hounded by creditors. The Micawber family, like the Dickens family, has a small servant taken from a workhouse who refers to herself as an "orfling". Mrs. Micawber ornaments the street-door with a brass plate which announces "Mrs. Micawber's Boarding Establishment for Young Ladies" – but she has no more success with it than Mrs. Dickens.

"The only visitors I ever saw or heard of," says David Copperfield, "were creditors. *They* used to come at all hours, and some of them were quite ferocious. One dirty-faced man, I think he was a boot-maker, used to edge himself into the passage as early as seven o'clock in the morning, and call up the stairs to Mr. Micawber – 'Come! You ain't out yet, you know. Pay us, will you? Don't hide, you know; that's mean. I wouldn't be mean if I was you. Pay us, will you? You just pay us, d'ye hear? Come!'"

David trudges on errands to pawnbrokers for the family, work that becomes intensified when Mr. Micawber is carried off to the King's Bench prison for debtors. Then Mrs. Micawber, the children and the "orfling" join him there. All the pitiful details of the Dickens family's distresses at this time can be filled in from the account of the Micawbers.

For the bottom strata of society there could be no question of debt or debtors' prisons. They lived from hand to mouth, from day to day; nobody would trust them with anything that they could not pay for immediately. Nor is it likely that they possessed much on which a pawnbroker would lend them anything. The higher one's position in society, the easier it became to live comfortably in the absence of money. Thus the Micawber family were never without food or shelter, however much their creditors pressed, while Thackeray's Crawleys, in *Vanity Fair*, surrounded with mountainous debts, lived like princes.

10 · Poverty and Destitution

THE state of the poor, de Tocqueville had said after his visit in 1833, was England's deepest trouble. Many Englishmen of the time would have agreed with him; all through the 30's and 40's they were watched uneasily, a savage mass who, maddened by hunger, might at any moment leap from their lairs and engulf the country in blood and fire.

The poor, of course, had always been a problem. There had always been the widowed and the fatherless, the aged and the infirm, the idler and the wastrel and those who might be dependent upon them. But with an industrial society there came a new problem: the able-bodied man whose work had been taken from him by machines, or who lost the work he had because of a slump in trade. Trade depressions in the "hungry forties" meant thousands of men unemployed, starving, their families with them. It was a problem that the Victorians never solved. They grappled with the evils arising out of poverty, rather than with why poverty occurs in the first place and how best to prevent it. And they tried to deal with it through local effort and private charity rather than tackle it on a national scale.

By the 1830's it was glaringly clear that the existing Poor Law, originally formulated in 1601, was quite inadequate to deal with the poor of the 19th century. The 17th century Poor Law had stipulated that the householders

Chapter heading from *Divine and Moral Songs for Children,* (1849 edition).

of each parish must contribute to a poor rate, and from this the poor and
the destitute of the parish (known as paupers) should be supported. But
the growth of cities in the industrial age and the people who crowded into
them from the country completely altered the situation. Which parish
should bear the burden of the newcomers who drifted round the towns,
seeking work? What parish was wealthy enough to cope with mass unem⁄
ployment?

In the country things were little better. The custom had been adopted
in many parishes of supplementing a man's wages out of the parish rates
if he could not earn enough to support himself and his family.[1] But what
had been intended as a humane measure turned out in fact a great evil.
Farmers no longer paid their men a living wage, they left it to the poor rates

"OUT OF THE PARISH!"

A *Punch* cartoon of 1865 showing a landowner ordering an aged labourer out of
the parish so that he will not have to be supported by the local poor rates.

1 Known as the Speenhamland System, and referred to as "outdoor relief," it had been
introduced by the magistrates of Speenhamland, Berkshire, to avert widespread famine
in 1795.

to provide for them. There was no incentive to the farm worker to be prudent or thrifty or industrious, since however hard he worked the poor rates would keep his wage to the lowest possible level. If he possessed anything, even a few pounds saved over the years, he was refused help from the parish, and without help from the parish no one would employ him. Farmers looked to the parish to help pay their wage bill, farm workers were reduced to paupers, and the land was breaking under the burden of the poor rate.

What was to be done? The political economist Thomas Malthus, who died in 1834, held that the poor should be suppressed. The earth, he considered, was over-populated, and charities and relief of those who could not support themselves only encouraged people to produce more children. They must be discouraged even if it meant starving them, otherwise the whole earth would be peopled with paupers. It was against this attitude that so many of Dickens's novels passionately protest.

This Malthusian teaching was widely accepted by the intellectuals of the time. Among them was Harriet Martineau,[1] who produced in 1833 a collection of stories under the title of *Poor Law and Paupers Illustrated* in which she set down her feelings about the evils of the Poor Law as it existed then. Put into the form of fiction, her views seem far more horrifying and unnatural than they might if expressed in the terser language of an economist. In *Cousin Marshall* one of her characters decides that he must give up his appointment as medical officer to the Lying-In Hospital and the Dispensary. "'There is enough harm done by the poor taking for granted that they are to be supplied with medicine and advice gratis all their lives: the evil is increasing every day by their looking on assistance in child-birth as their due; and if they learn to expect food and warmth in like manner, their misery will be complete.'" He allows that the blind, deaf and dumb should be cared for in asylums and that accidents should be treated free. But any provision for the old is very bad, because it encourages people to marry (and thereby have children) far too young, and to shrug off the burden of their aged relations. The surgeon solemnly warns his sister that unless speedy steps are taken England will become a "vast congregation of paupers . . . twenty-four millions of paupers bound by law to maintain twenty-four millions of paupers."

Miss Martineau put her case with considerable vehemence, perhaps,

1 Harriet Martineau (1802–76). Writer on social reform and political economy, and of stories illustrating these.

but her views were those of many people who had tried to think the matter out rationally, and Malthusian teaching accounts for the unfeeling attitude towards the poor that modern readers often detect in 19th century writers. The problem of the poor was so horrible and so immense that it was easier to shelter behind the theories of Malthus and his followers than to seek other solutions. The poor, said a large body of opinion, should exert them-selves, be thrifty, save for old age and sickness; Dickens was to attack this attitude with savage irony again and again.

In 1833 – the same year that Harriet Martineau brought out her moral tales – the Commissioners appointed to report on the Poor Law stated that outdoor relief acted as "a national provision for discouraging the honest and industrious, and protecting the lazy, vicious, and improvident," that it encouraged early marriage and large families. Their findings con-firmed what most people had thought, that the Poor Law as it existed must be changed to deal more effectively with the fearful problem of the poor of England. In 1834, as a result of their recommendations, the new Poor Law came into being, the Poor Law to which constant reference is made in the Victorian novel, which cast a shadow over the lives of millions and which kept its power to frighten for a century and more. By the provi-sions of the 1834 Poor Law relief outside the workhouse was to be kept to the barest minimum; they might starve outside it, or they might enter within and receive food in return for work. Parishes were to unite and set up "union" workhouses to serve the whole district (the local workhouse was often referred to as the "union" after this), which were to be governed by a local Board of Guardians.

"The workhouse," wrote Engels in *The Condition of the Working-Class in 1844* "has been made the most repulsive residence which the refined ingenuity of a Malthusiasn can invent. The food is worse than that of the most ill-paid working man while employed, and the work harder, or they might prefer the workhouse to their own wretched existence outside. . . . The food of criminal prisoners is better, as a rule, so that the paupers frequently commit some offence for the purpose of getting into jail. For the workhouse is a jail too; he who does not finish his task gets nothing to eat; he who wishes to go out must ask permission, which is granted or not, according to his behaviour or the inspector's whim; tobacco is forbidden, also the receipt of gifts from relatives or friends outside the house; the paupers wear a workhouse uniform, and are handed over, helpless and without redress, to the caprice of the inspectors. To prevent their labour from competing with that of outside concerns, they are set to rather useless tasks: the men break stones, 'as much as a strong man can accomplish with effort in a day;' the women, children and aged men pick oakum,[1] for I know not what insigni-ficant use. To prevent the 'superfluous' from multiplying, and 'demoral-ized' parents from influencing their children, families are broken up; the husband is placed in one wing, the wife in another, the children in a third, and they are permitted to see one another only at stated times after long intervals, and then only when they have, in the opinion of the officials, behaved well. And in order to shut off the external world from contamina-tion with pauperism within these bastilles, the inmates are permitted to receive visits only with the consent of the officials, and in the reception rooms; to communicate in general with the world outside by leave and under supervision."

Engels goes on to give examples of young children being punished by being shut into the dead-room where they had to sleep upon the lids of coffins; of tramps shut up naked in a hole under the stairs for eight or ten days on end; of a man of 72 sent to the tread-mill for two weeks for refusing, on the grounds of his old age, to break stones.

Oliver Twist, which originally appeared in instalments between 1837 and 1838, is by far the best known of all the protests about the administration of the new Poor Law, and is made particularly striking by the heavy irony of the style:

"When [the board] came to turn their attention to the workhouse, they found out at once, what ordinary folks would never have discovered – the poor people liked it! It was a regular place of public entertainment for the poorer classes; a tavern where there was nothing to pay; a public breakfast, dinner, tea, and supper all the year round; a brick and mortar elysium, where it was all play and no work. 'Oho!' said the board, looking very knowing; 'we are the fellows to set this to rights; we'll stop it all, in no time.' So, they established the rule, that all poor people should have the alternative (for they would compel nobody, not they), of being starved by a gradual process in the house, or by a quick one out of it. With this view,

1 Oakum picking and other prison occupations of the time are described on p. 215.

A YOUNG PAUPER REBELS

George Cruickshank's illustration of the scene in the workhouse when Oliver
Twist asks for more gruel.

they contracted with the water-works to lay on an unlimited supply of
water; and with a corn-factor to supply periodically small quantities of
oatmeal; and issued three meals of gruel a day, with an onion twice a week,
and half a roll on Sundays. They made a great many other wise and humane
regulations, having reference to the ladies, which it is not necessary to
repeat; kindly undertook to divorce poor married people, in consequence
of the great expense of a suit in Doctor's Commons; and, instead of com-
pelling a man to support his family, as they had theretofore done, took his
family away from him, and made him a bachelor! There is no saying how
many applicants for relief, under these last two heads, might have started

up in all classes of society, if it had not been coupled with the workhouse; but the board were long-headed men, and had provided for this difficulty. The relief was inseparable from the workhouse and the gruel; and that frightened people."

People were indeed frightened. The shadow of the workhouse awaiting them at the end of their lives, threatening to overtake them if they were too infirm to work or could find none, hung over all the Victorian poor, and most of them would go to any lengths to avoid 'the house'. Many Victorians inferred from this that few of the so-called destitute were in fact in dire need. A writer no doubt reflected the attitude of many of his con-temporaries in 1879 when he pointed out that of 647 people who applied for relief only 27 accepted the condition of workhouse residence, and con-cluded that there could not therefore have been real distress in the case of the other 620.[1]

Taine was shown a workhouse in Manchester. He reported that it was well-planned, clean and well run. There was a pleasant outlook of trees and fields, an abundance of fresh air.

"Beside the row of hovels in which the poor live, this place is a palace.... Yet at the time of writing there is not one able-bodied person to be found in a workhouse: the one that we saw is almost empty and will only be filled when winter comes. As a rule, when a workman out of a job applies to the municipality for help he is told, 'Give us proof that you are willing to work: go to the workhouse.' Nine times out of ten the men refuse. What is the reason for this repugnance? I saw, today, an old woman sorting through a heap of rubbish, and picking out remnants of vegetables with her thin hands: she may have been one of those who are unwilling to give up their drop of gin. But what of the others? I am told that they will stick to their 'home' and their liberty at any price and cannot bear to be shut up and become subject to discipline. 'They prefer to be free and so starve.'"

Dickens's great example of the wish to be free and to starve is Betty Higden in *Our Mutual Friend*, whose single aim is to keep out of the hands of the Relieving Officer and the workhouse. Feeling death close to her she wanders over the country with the money to pay for her burial sewn into her gown.

1 T. H. S. Escott: *England: its People, Polity, and Pursuits.*

"If she could wear through the day, and then lie down to die under the cover of the darkness, she would die independent. If she were captured previously, the money would be taken from her as a pauper who had no right to it, and she would be carried to the accursed workhouse."

She sees phantoms of Relieving Officers all round her, hunting her down, in order to drag her off as a pauper to die in a pauper ward. "It is a remarkable Christian improvement," comments Dickens, "to have made a pursuing Fury of the Good Samaritan."

Our Mutual Friend first appeared 1864-5; in the 1860's there were plenty of real examples of horrifying hardship suffered under the Poor Law. Humphry House in *The Dickens World* quotes from a coroner's report on a woman who had died from starvation:

"It was clear that the deceased and her family, being in extreme starvation, presented herself at the union house. . . . They were placed in a room and there had to undergo such dreadful starvation that deceased died of the effects, and they would have all perished had not their groans attracted the atten tion of the neighbours."

This was an extreme case, no doubt, where the Relieving Officer had neglected his duty; the Poor Law did not normally expect to starve paupers into their graves. But it exacted a great deal from them in the way of work and humiliation before it consented to relieve their distress.

James Greenwood, a journalist whose articles on his experiences in the casual ward of a London workhouse had aroused much feeling in 1866, described in *The Wilds of London* (1874) the labours that were demanded from men who applied for relief at workhouses. If they were fit enough, they were set to breaking stones; while young boys and old men picked oakum – that is, they were given a set amount of ships' rope, saturated with tar and hard as wood, which had to be shredded into pieces small enough to be used to caulk ships' timbers. Both tasks could be per formed far more quickly and economically by machine, said Greenwood, but what angered him most was the sight of "the sturdy villain – the parish rover and vagabond by profession – earning with ease enough at least to buy him bread to eat, and beer to drink, and tobacco to smoke, while the hundred times more deserving, but weak bodied and soft handed out o'

WORKHOUSE WARD, 1847

This newly completed ward at Marylebone workhouse was regarded as a model of its kind. The scripture texts, painted in red letters on a blue ground, were thought particularly suitable. (*Illustrated London News.*)

work tailor, or baker, or clerk, is sweating under the rags of his old respectability and straining his unused muscles that he may carry home a dry loaf to his children."

Nor did all workhouses make equal demands from the people who applied for relief. At one London parish stoneyard, for instance, the overseer would not give one halfpenny until a man had broken his full half-yard of stone, while other overseers paid according to the amount done. The administration of the Poor Law varied enormously from district to district according to the humanity and efficiency of the authorities. Dickens concluded *Our Mutual Friend* with a comment on this:

"I believe there has been in England, since the days of the Stuarts, no law so often infamously administered, no law so often openly violated, no law habitually so ill-supervised. In the majority of the shameful cases of disease and death from destitution that shock the Public and disgrace the country, the illegality is quite equal to the inhumanity – and known language could say no more of their lawlessness."

Until society had learned to deal with the problem of the unemployed, and until the working man was certain of a minimum living wage, there was bound to be terrible hardship. The worst conditions of the Poor Law were improved as the century progressed, but Old Age Pensions, which aimed at keeping the aged poor out of the workhouses, were not introduced until the beginning of the 20th century, and national schemes for providing against ill-health and unemployment came later still. Throughout the 19th century it was commonly held that the working classes if only they were careful enough, could provide out of their savings against sickness, old age, and unemployment.

But wages in the 19th century were rarely enough to allow the lower-paid working man to save. Charles Kingsley in *Yeast* speaks passionately of the exhausting toil that a labourer must endure just to scrape together enough money to feed and house his family. The gamekeeper explains this to the gentleman who has never been called upon to work for his living:

"Men that write books and talk at elections call this a free country, and say that the poorest and meanest has a free opening to rise and become prime minister, if he can. But you see, sir, the misfortune is, that in practice he can't; for one who gets into a gentleman's family, or into a little shop, and so saves a few pounds, fifty know that they've no chance before them, but day-labourer born, day-labourer live, from hand to mouth, scraping and pinching to get not meat and beer even, but bread and potatoes; and then, at the end of it all, for a worthy reward, half-a-crown a week of parish pay – or the workhouse. That's a lively hopeful prospect for a Christian man!"

How did the poor then, contrive to keep out of the workhouse if they could not find work? In the towns they begged by day, or scounged for scraps that they could eat or sell. At night they might huddle under a railway arch, shivering with cold, and afraid that the policeman with his bulls-eye

ASLEEP UNDER THE STARS
The homeless in London sleeping on the Embankment. Engraving by Doré
(*London,* 1872).

lantern would come and move them on. All foreign visitors to England in the earlier decades of Victoria's reign commented on the hideousness of the poverty that they saw there, particularly in London, and on the throngs of beggars in the streets. "Certainly the vile and horrible are worse in this country than elsewhere," said Taine, describing a walk through the dock area of Shadwell in East London in 1858.

"From the moment you emerge . . . the whole place is alive with 'street-boys', bare-footed, filthy, turning cartwheels for a penny. They swarm on the stairs down to the Thames, more stunted, more livid, more deformed, more repulsive than the street urchins of Paris; the climate, of course, is worse, and the gin murderous. Among them, leaning against the festering walls, or crouched inert on the steps, are men in the most astonishing rags: nobody who has not seen them can conceive what a frock-coat or pair of trousers can carry in layers of filth. They doze and day-dream, their faces earthy, livid, marbled with fine red lines. It was in this quarter that families were discovered whose only bed was a heap of soot; they had been sleeping on it for some months. For the human being reduced to these conditions there is only one refuge: drunkenness."

There were abundant studies of the atrocious conditions of the poor made by journalists and clergy in the 1850's and 60's. The most famous and most detailed of these is undoubtedly Henry Mayhew's *London Labour and the London Poor* which was published in four volumes in 1861–2. It took him nearly fifteen years to amass all this material, during which he and his collaborators tramped London, talking to beggars, vagrants, thieves, street hawkers, street performers, scroungers and scavengers of all sorts, as well as working men. He sets down, very often in their own words, the pathetic details of their lives, and their work should they be lucky enough to have any. There are the old, the crippled, widows and orphans, struggling to earn a few pence, just enough to keep them from starvation that day – they have not the strength to plan for the day after. Some sweep the crossings, others hawk small wares, or comb the mud by the Thames for bits of coal or nails that they can sell for food. Some even collect dog dung from the streets which they sell to the tan-yards for curing leather. Mayhew speaks to a lame old woman who has given up hawking tapes and cottons to tend her dying husband, though she has nothing to feed him upon but warm sugar and water flavoured with cinnamon.

"'What shocked him most was that I was obligated in his old age to go and ask for relief at the parish. You see, he was always a spiritful man, and it hurted him sorely that he should come to this at last, and for the first time in his lifetime. The only parish money that ever we had was this, and it *does* hurt him every day to think that he must be buried by the parish after all. He was always proud, you see."

An eighty-year-old crossing-sweeper, deaf and feeble, whose husband is dead and sons transported, goes out every morning to sweep her crossing and catch the workmen on their way to the factories:

"I goes every morning, winter or summer, frost or snow; and at the same hour (five o'clock); people certainly don't think of giving so much in fine weather. Nobody ever mislested me, and I never mislested nobody. If they gives me a penny, I thanks 'em; and if they gives me nothing, I thanks 'em all the same.

"If I was to go into the House, I shouldn't live three days. It's not that I eat much – a very little is enough for me; but it's the air I should miss: to be shut up like a thief, I couldn't live long, I know."

A CROSSING-SWEEPER
Henry Mayhew: *London Labour and the London Poor,* 1861–2.

Mayhew also investigated the beggars, of whom there were enormous numbers in London at that time. Begging, in fact, was a profession on its own account, and Mayhew listed some of the types to be seen in the streets.

"Of the beggars there are many distinct species. (1) The naval and the military beggars; as turnpike sailors and 'raw' veterans. (2) Distressed operative beggars; as pretended starved-out manufacturers, or sham frozen-out gardeners, or tricky hand-loom weavers. (3) Respectable beggars; as sham broken-down tradesmen, poor ushers, or distressed authors, clean family beggars, with children in very white pinafores and their faces cleanly washed, and the ashamed beggars, who pretend to hide their faces with a written petition. (4) Disaster beggars; as shipwrecked mariners, or blown-up miners, or burnt-out tradesmen, and lucifer droppers.[1] (5) Bodily afflicted beggars; such as those having real or pretended sores

1 These, often children, tried to awake the pity of passersby by pretending to have dropped all the matches they hoped to sell.

or swollen legs, or being crippled or deformed, maimed, or paralyzed, or else being blind, or deaf, or dumb, or subject to fits, or in a decline and appearing with bandages round the head, or playing the 'shallow cove', i.e., appearing half-clad in the streets. (6) Famished beggars; as those who chalk on the pavement, 'I am starving,' or else remain stationary, and hold up a piece of paper before their face similarly inscribed. (7) Foreign beggars who stop you in the street, and request to know if you can speak French; or destitute Poles, Indians, or Lascars, or Negroes. (8) Petty trading beggars; as tract sellers, lucifer match sellers, boot-lace vendors, &c. (9) Musical beggars; or those who play on some musical instrument, as a cloak for begging – as scraping fiddlers, hurdy-gurdy and clarionet players. (10) Dependents of beggars; as screevers or the writers of 'slums' (letters), and 'fakements' (petitions), and referees, or those who give characters to professional beggars."

The last category in Mayhew's list shows how organized begging had become. Nor did it stop at beggars employing letter writers, they also made use of baby agencies, where they could hire a few children and infants in arms, to add colour to stories about destitute families. The *Quarterly Review* reported a conversation between two women who had hired children.

"How much did you give for yours?"
"A shilling a-piece."
"A shilling a-piece! – Vy then you've been done, or babbies is riz; one or t'other – I only give sixpence for mine, and they feeds 'em and Godfrey's-cordials 'em and all, afore I takes 'em, into the bargain!"

Beggars and criminals lived side by side in the London rookeries, and very often there might be no clear distinction between the two. The cadging beggar might snatch up a few portable objects from the kitchen of the house where he had gone begging; his children no doubt would follow the example of those they saw round them and turn into pickpockets. The beggars, according to some reports, moved about in gangs. An inspector of lodging houses in the notorious St. Giles area of London spoke of a beggars' kitchen in a lodging house there. They fed richly, he said, on the food they had cadged from wealthy kitchens, or bought with the alms they had begged. "In the morning they often sat down to a breakfast of tea,

MOVING THEM ON
The policeman with his bull's eye lantern shifts a huddle of homeless wanderers
from their shelter under a wall. Engraving by Doré (*London*, 1872).

coffee, eggs, rashers of bacon, dried fish, fresh butter, and other good things, which would be considered luxuries by working people, when each dis-cussed his plans for the day's rambles, and arranged as to the exchange of garments, bandages, &c., considered necessary to prevent recognition in those neighbourhoods recently 'worked'."

Stories such as these made the Victorian public very wary. As early as 1818 the upper classes had tried to protect themselves against the "undeserv-ing poor" by forming a Mendicity Society. Subscribers gave the funds they would otherwise have given direct to beggars, to the Society instead, and sent the people who asked their help to the Society to have their cases investigated.

"The upper classes, the swells, ain't so good, they subscribe to the Mendicity Society," a beggar told Mayhew, "and they thinks every beggar an im-posture. The half-and-half swells, shopmen and the likes, ain't got no hearts, and they ain't got no money, and what's the good. Tradesmen that ain't over well off have a fellow feeling; but the workmen's wives out a-marketing of a Saturday night are no trouble. They always carries coppers – change out of sixpence or a something – in their hands, and when I goes in where they are a havin' their daffies – that's drops o' gin, sir – they looks at me, and says 'Poor man!' and drops the coppers, whatever it is, into my hand, and p'raps asks me to take a half-pint o' beer besides. They're good souls, the workmen's wives."

Dickens would have warmed to these comments. In all his novels he shows enthusiastic approval for spontaneous, open-handed generosity, and suspicion of the organized charity that was a feature of the Victorian age. The 19th century saw the launching of fleets of charitable institutions. Out of a total of 640 institutions in 1862, 279 were founded in the first 50 years of the century and 144 between 1850 and that date. They covered an enormously wide field; there were orphanages, almshouses, dispensaries, and hospitals; societies to provide coal, blankets, potatoes, shoes, religious literature, surgical appliances, linen for women in childbirth. It has been remarked that what began in the early decades of the century as the action of frightened upper classes trying to protect themselves against the terrifying poverty they saw about them and the revolution it might bring, was con-tinued by the mid-Victorians out of routine 'good form'. To subscribe to a certain number of charities was considered the respectable thing to do. It also protected the donor against imposters, for the Victorians drew sharp distinction between the 'deserving' and the 'undeserving' poor, and it was assumed that the charities would sort the sheep from the goats.

Dickens drew attention to the way snobbery played a large part in the giving; people could be tempted to subscribe to a society if they thought thereby their names might be linked with a nobleman's. Mr. Boffin in *Our Mutual Friend* receives a "large fat private double letter, sealed with a ducal coronet," inviting him to subscribe three guineas to a charity and to sit down at a dinner at which that duke is presiding. Two noble earls and a viscount ask him to present a purse of one hundred pounds to the Society for Granting Annuities to Unassuming Members of the Middle Classes.

Dickens reserves his deadliest shafts against organized charity for two characters in *Bleak House*, Mrs. Jellyby and Mrs. Pardiggle. Mrs. Jellyby is "a lady of very remarkable strength of character, who devotes herself entirely to the public . . . and is at present (until something else attracts her)

A CHARITY BANQUET

Girls from Welsh charity schools (their hair cropped as befitted charity girls) are paraded past subscribers, who include the Prince of Wales. From *The Illustrated London News*, 1867.

devoted to the subject of Africa." While she sits calmly dictating letters about the cultivation of the coffee berry and the education of the natives of Borrioboola-Gha her unfortunate children, dirty and untended, tumble downstairs and get their heads stuck in the area railings, quite unheeded. Mrs. Pardiggle specializes in charitable works nearer home. She disapproves of Mrs. Jellyby's treatment of her children, who are not sufficiently encouraged to participate in charitable activities. Mrs. Pardiggle prides herself that her children do this, though the narrator's comment is that she has never seen such ferociously discontented children. Each of the five boys frowned savagely when their mother said complacently how they had sacrificed their pocket money to contribute to charitable causes.

In company with Mrs. Pardiggle the two heroines of *Bleak House* go to visit a brickmaker and his family in their wretched little hovel on a brick-field. Visiting the poor was by no means fiction. Energetic and conscientious middle class women, particularly the wives and daughters of the clergy, made a practice of it. They would advise and exhort, read the Bible to the sick and the aged, urge mothers to send their children to Sunday school and to bring the latest baby to be baptized, counsel thrift, and give practical help in the way of baby-clothes, or food for an invalid. They find the brickmaker ferocious in his misery.

"I wants an end of these liberties took with my place. I wants an end of being drawed like a badger. Now you're a-going to poll-pry and question according to custom – I know what you're a-going to be up to. Well! You haven't got no occasion to be up to it. I'll save you the trouble. Is my daughter a-washin? Yes, she *is* a-washin. Look at the water. Smell it! that's wot we drinks. How do you like it, and what do you think of gin, instead! An't my place dirty? Yes, it is dirty – it's nat'rally dirty, and it's nat'rally onwhole-some; and we've had five firty and onwholesome children, as is all dead infants, and so much the better for them, and for us besides. Have I read the little book wot you left? No, I an't read the little book wot you left. There an't nobody here as knows how to read it; and if there wos, it wouldn't be suitable to me. It's a book fit for a babby, and I'm not a babby. If you was to leave me a doll, I shouldn't nuss it. How have I been conducting of myself? Why, I've been drunk for three days; and I'd a been drunk four, if I'd a had the money. Don't I never mean for to go to church? No, I don't never mean for me to go to church. I shouldn't be expected there if I did; the

MRS. PARDIGGLE TAKES HER CHILDREN TO VISIT THE
BRICKMAKER'S COTTAGE
An illustration from *Bleak House*.

beadle's too gen-teel for me. And how did my wife get that black eye?
Why, I giv' it her; and if she says I didn't, she's a Lie."

While Mrs. Pardiggle and the two girls, Esther and Ada, are visiting this
family the brickmaker's baby, ailing and feeble, dies in its mother's arms.
Esther and Ada, moved by genuine love and pity, weep and try to comfort
the poor mother. Their behaviour is used by Dickens as a rebuke to the
Mrs. Pardiggles of his time who, secure in their middle-class comfort and
respectability, try to preach middle-class virtues to people whose problems
and difficulties they make little attempt to understand, and for whom they
feel no real compassion.

11 · Criminals

"'THE Jago's got you,'" an old man tells the small boy in *A Child of the Jago*, a story of a young thief in the Bethnal Green area of London. He points out to him the High Mobsmen – the flourishing and successful criminals – strutting round the Jago, and tells him bitterly that he had better try to imitate them. "'There it is – that's your aim in life – there's your pattern. Learn to read and write, learn all you can, learn cunning, spare nobody and stop at nothing . . . It's the best the world has for you, for the Jago's got you, and that's the only way out, except the gaol and the gallows.'"

Arthur Morrison wrote this little known novel of poverty and crime in 1896. For decades Victorian writers had spoken eloquently on this very point. Newspaper articles, sermons, pamphlets, tract tales for children had described in vivid and horrifying detail the abysses of poverty that existed in the great cities, from which crime inevitably sprang. Lord Shaftesbury, some fifty years earlier, had estimated that there were "30,000 naked, filthy, roaming, lawless children, who formed the seed plot of nineteen-twentieths of the crime which desolates the metropolis." There had been reforms which sought to improve living conditions; something has been said about these in chapter eight. But even in the late 19th century whole tracts of London remained in which all the inhabitants were criminal, more or less, and where it was impossible for a child to grow up uncorrupted, and nearly as impossible for him to earn an honest livelihood.

Chapter heading from *Divine and Moral Songs for Children*, (1849 edition).

Arthur Morrison's novels stand out among all the flood of Victorian writing about crime because of their sober, factual reporting of a way of life that seemed natural and inevitable to those who lived it. Harrison Ainsworth[1] made crime heroic and romantic; Wilkie Collins[2] made it seem fantastic. Dickens, fascinated by it, wrote of it (as V. S. Pritchett remarked) with a "sadistic touch of angry ecstasy." Arthur Morrison recorded what he had seen and left comment to others.

The "child" of the title is Dicky Perrott, the Jago one of the foulest of the London rookeries. His father was once a plasterer, but now carries a cosh, and the family lives on what he can plunder from his coshed victims. No stranger ventures into the Jago unless he is drunk; he will be attacked and stripped if he does. No law is enforced there, the police do not enter except in strong bands. Street wars rage up and down the foul and noisome courts; the police only step in when a man is killed.

Dicky picks his first pocket when he is nine and bears back a gold watch in triumph to his parents, who beat him for it, and sell the watch. Dicky sees theft as part of one's everyday life – how could you eat otherwise? "'It's the mugs wot git took,'" he says to his mother, "'and quoddin' ain't so bad. ... S'pose father'll be smugged some day, eh, mother?'" A clergyman finds him a job in a hardware shop, but this only lasts for a few days, for the publican who has been making a nice profit out of the stolen goods Dicky has brought him, and who resents his newfound honesty, brings about his downfall. Dicky makes no further efforts in the direction of honesty. He drifts along with the other Jago boys in a life of petty theft; but for him it is more serious than it is with some, for his father is now in prison, and his mother and the baby will starve unless he brings something home each night. It is a commonplace in the Jago that whatever somebody else has is yours if you are strong enough to take it, and fast enough to get clear away with it. What would have become of Dicky in adult life is left untold. He is stabbed in one of the street fights when he is seventeen, a week after his father has been hanged for murder.

From children such as this sprang the professional criminal. They had been carried into the beershops and gin palaces by their mothers in their

1 William Harrison Ainsworth (1805–82). Author of historical romances of which *The Tower of London* and *Old St. Paul's* are among the best known.

2 William Wilkie Collins (1824–89). Author of *The Moonstone* and *The Woman in White*. Regarded as the first writer of detective fiction.

THIEVES GAMBLING
Engraving by Doré (*London,* 1872).

earliest infancy; clothed in rags they had begged beside them, or hawked goods in the streets, snatching and stealing what they could. Many of them had no parents. As young children they were likely to be sneak-thieves, purloining from shops, snatching objects from the houses where they went to beg, knocking down smaller children sent on errands and robbing them of a few coppers. As they grew older they branched off into their own particular line. There were those who stayed sneak thieves all their lives; others became expert pickpockets, some were ultimately to be house-breakers.

Pickpockets swarmed in the streets of Victorian cities. They might be ragged urchins filching handkerchiefs from the tails of men's coats, or elegantly dressed experts who promenaded in the West End and attended fashionable assemblies. Some were dressed as mechanics, others as clerks, smart business men, or men of fashion. They were trained as Fagin trained his boys and attempted to train Oliver Twist, by men who taught them their trade, sent them out into the streets, and disposed of the property that they brought back. Mayhew described their lessons: "A coat is suspended on the wall with a bell attached to it, and the boy attempts to take the hand-kerchief from the pocket without the bell ringing. . . . Another way they are trained is this: the trainer – if a man – walks up and down the room with a handkerchief in the tail of his coat, and the ragged boys amuse themselves abstracting it until they learn to do it in an adroit manner."

Professional thief-trainers such as Fagin were a commonplace, long after Dickens wrote *Oliver Twist*. James Greenwood, who wrote much about mid-Victorian poverty and crime, quoted in *The Seven Curses of London* (1869) from the experience of a clergyman:

"In every low criminal neighbourhood there are numbers of children who never knew their parents, and who are fed and clothed by the old thieves, and made to earn their wages by dishonest practices. When the parent thieves are imprisoned or transported, their children are left to shift for themselves, and so fall into the hands of the thief-trainer. . . . Sharpened by hunger, intimidated by severe treatment, and rendered adroit by vigilant training, this class of thieves is perhaps the most daring, the cleverest, and the most difficult to reform. . . . The poor helpless little children literally grow up into a criminal career, and have no means of knowing that they are wrong.

"They have an ingrained conviction that it is *you* who are wrong, not them. That you are wrong in the first place in appropriating all the good things the world affords, leaving none for them but what they steal; and in the next place, they regard all your endeavours to persuade them to abandon

A WHITECHAPEL COFFEE HOUSE

Blanchard Jerrold and his companions visit a common haunt of thieves. Engraving by Doré (*London, 1872*).

the wretched life of a thief for the equally poor though more creditable existence of the honest lad as humbug and selfishness. . . . They believe the clergy are all hypocrites, the judges and magistrates tyrants, and honest people their bitterest enemies."

The common lodging houses in the great cities undoubtedly acted as a forcing house for crime. They existed in the poorest areas, and gave shelter to anyone who could pay a couple of coppers. The city streets swarmed with the homeless and destitute. If they could beg or steal or earn a few pence they took themselves to a lodging house; they could cook such food as they had by the fire there, and stretch themselves out for the night. Blanchard Jerrold, who toured these areas of London in 1872 (with a strong police escort) in the company of the artist Gustave Doré with whom he collaborated in *London, a pilgrimage* – from which some of the illustrations to this book are taken, described a tour of some of London's lodging houses. They were shown long, low rooms, partitioned by deal boarding into small compart/

ments each holding a bed for which the occupant would be charged two-pence. Always there hung over the place "the unmistakable, overpowering damp and mouldy odour, that is in every thieves' kitchen, in every common lodging house, every ragged hotel." The lodgers crouched in corners eating scraps, huddled round the fire, quarrelled, played cards, the girl who had come in for shelter mixing with the prostitute from the White-chapel road, young boys with known thieves. The policeman who escorted the party commented on this. Once they had come here, he said, they were lost. It was impossible, mixing like this, for the innocent to stay uncorrupted. They might fight against it, but unless they could afford to leave the lodging houses, it was useless. "But you see, there's no place for them as cheap as this."

The prisons no less than the lodging houses helped sow seeds of crime. Mayhew, collecting material for *The Criminal Prisons of London* (1862) visited Tothill Fields. Up to 1850 it had been a local prison under the control of the Middlesex magistrates, but after this date – and thus at the time that Mayhew visited it – it was restricted to female prisoners and boys under the age of seventeen. It was a house of correction – that is, it held short-term prisoners – and it stood in the "Devil's Acre", the moral plague spot of the whole kingdom, a contemporary called it – behind the Houses of Parliament. Mayhew found 271 boys there, 177 of whom were shut up at night for twelve and a half hours in tiny stone-floored cells, unheated, unlit, without any means of calling a warder in an emergency, and without any proper ventilation, some of the windows being unglazed and only shuttered at night. The boys spent six hours a day in picking oakum, and two and three-quarter hours in exercising, chapel, and schooling.

"True, the place is called a house of correction; but, rightly viewed, it is simply a criminal preparatory school, where students are qualified for matriculating at Millbank or Pentonville.[1] Here we find little creatures of six years of age branded with a felon's badge – boys, not even in their teens, clad in the prison dress, for the heinous offence of throwing stones, or obstructing highways, or unlawfully knocking at doors – crimes which the very magistrates themselves, who committed the youths, must have

[1] Millbank Penitentiary and Pentonville were both convict prisons which held prisoners with long sentences.

assuredly perpetuated in their boyhood, and which, if equally visited would consign almost every child in the kingdom to a jail."

Certainly most of the schoolboys at Thomas Hughes' Rugby would have found themselves in jail. Tom Brown and his friends swarm over the countryside, setting night-lines for fish, poaching duck, stealing birds' nests, peppering passers-by with their pea-shooters, and behaving with lordly insolence to the gamekeepers and farmers who try to stop them. But lawless conduct such as this was generally regarded as manly and normal in the upper classes. If a street arab or a farm labourer's child were caught at such enormities he would be thrust into a house of correction, or the local gaol, and there was little hope of his being able to earn an honest living when he came out.

The journalist James Greenwood had his own theory to contribute on the cause of juvenile crime of the period. He repeatedly claimed that the "gallows literature" glorifying crime was largely to blame. In *The Seven Curses of London* he states that he bought, for curiosity, "six poison-pen'orths" of this from a small newspaper vendor in Clerkenwell. It included such titles as *The Skeleton Band, Tyburn Dick, The Black Knight of the Road, Dick Turpin, The Boy Burglar*, and *Starlight Sall*. Publishers, said Greenwood hotly, had even been known to distribute daggers with certain issues, and he stated that at least half the young thieves in gaol admitted they had been led astray by such literature, and tempted to follow the example of "such gallows heroes as Dick Turpin and Blueskin."

He confessed, however, that you had to be cautious when listening to young criminals, and gave an instance of a prison governor who was convinced that literature of this sort was the mainspring of juvenile crime, and equally certain that the best way to break a bad boy was to speak to him of his mother. Greenwood was conducted round the prison by this governor, who stopped at the "dark cell" (a much-dreaded cell where every glimmer of light was excluded, used for the solitary confinement of tough cases) and called out "a depraved and hardened little wretch" who had been dispatched there as punishment.

"*Governor*: Can you read, lad?

Lad: (with a penitential wriggle). Yes, sir; I wish as I couldn't, sir.

Governor: Ah! Why so?

Lad: (with a doleful wag of his bullet head). Cos then I shouldn't have

read none of them highwaymen's books, sir; it was them as was the beginning of it.

  Governor: Ah! (a pause). Have you a mother, my lad?

  Lad: Boo-oh!"

Greenwood is sceptical about the boy's sobs, but not so the governor,
who wags his finger at him and releases him from further punishment.

  The savagery of the earlier attitude towards criminals was easing by the
beginning of Victoria's reign. In 1814 a man was hanged for cutting down
a cherry tree, and a boy aged nine was hanged in 1831 for setting fire to a house.
But after 1832 murder, in practice, became virtually the only crime to be
punished by death. The last beheading after hanging took place in 1820,
and in 1832 the custom of publicly dissecting the bodies of certain hanged
criminals was stopped.

  There were notable changes too in the prison system. The old rule had
been a haphazard one, where incredible laxity and carelessness was combined with bestial living conditions and ferocious punishment. There
had been no national prison system; prisons were under the control of the

local magistrates, and therefore varied enormously from locality to locality, according to the dilgence and good sense of those in charge. By the 1830's a start had already been made with bringing some order and decency into prison conditions, and the Victorians gave much zealous and earnest attention to the whole system of punishment. The system that they evolved may seem exceedingly harsh to us now, but this was not through neglect or indifference, as it had been fifty years earlier. On the contrary, there was a steady stream, throughout the reign, of Royal Commissions and Select Committees to inquire into one aspect or another of the treatment of crime; of reforms, and the publication of papers, pamphlets, and articles on the subject. Prisons were built in great numbers – indeed most of the existing buildings date from the Victorian age.

There were in the first fifty years of the century three ways in which one could punish a criminal. He could be hanged, he could be transported, or he could be imprisoned. By the 1830's, as we have seen, hanging was reserved for cases of murder, though the death-sentence was frequently pronounced on criminals whom the law had no intention of hanging and later reprieved.

Transportation had been in force since the times of James I when the king ordered 100 "dissolute persons" to be sent out to Virginia. Some 50,000 convicts were dispatched to America before the Declaration of Independence put an end to the practice. With America lost to them, the government had to look elsewhere, and in 1787 it sent the first shiploads to Australia, a place so convenient that it was not finally abandoned for the purpose until 1867. Australia as it became more settled protested at what it regarded as a tide of sewage poured upon its shores, and there was strong feeling among penal reformers in England which led, some time before 1867, to the gradual running down of the system. But if convicts were not to be shipped overseas, they would have to be housed at home, and in the first half of the century the country did not possess the prison accommoda-tion to hold them.

The original convicts dispatched to New South Wales remained in the hands of the government, in a penal colony inhabited only by the con-victs and their custodians. But as time went on, this system was agreed to be both costly and inconvenient. Laws were becoming milder and more humane at home which resulted in more prisoners escaping the gallows and reaching Australia instead. New South Wales was now attracting

THE AUSTRALIAN COLONIST AND THE CONVICTS
Colonist. "Now, Mr. Bull! Don't shoot any more of your Rubbish here, or you
and I shall quarrel." Cartoon from *Punch,* 1864.

free settlers and advancing in wealth and prosperity, and a new scheme
was devised to replace the old penal colony which had had the costly task
of feeding and housing and maintaining all the thousands of convicts
who reached Australia.

The government announced that it would freely lend its convicts to
anybody who would relieve them of the burden of supporting them. There
soon grew keen competition for convict labour. They were employed not
only as agricultural labourers on farmlands in the interior, but those who
had a trade or a profession were eagerly sought for work in the towns. Some
grew rich and prospered. Abel Magwitch, the convict in Dickens' *Great
Expectations* (written 1860–1 but referring to conditions in about 1830)
is one of these. From his sheep station in New South Wales he sends money
that he has earned and inherited from his master back to England to be
paid out to Pip, the little boy who tried to help him escape when he was a
prisoner on the hulks. His burning wish is to educate the boy to be a gentle-

man. Finally he comes to England with a full pocket book "fur to see my gentleman spend his money *like* a gentleman." But he comes back at the peril of his life, for if found, he will be hanged. England does not in the least care what a convict gets up to in Australia, but will not have him back home.

Magwitch was one of the more fortunate, chosen by a good master, for many of the employers who applied for convict labour were bad characters, who may well have been convicts themselves at an earlier stage. When they could not manage a man they sent him to the authorities to be flogged; a hopeless case was returned to government charge and might be set to work on the roads or in a chain gang – where he would have a military guard, be shackled with heavy leg irons and liable to instant flogging at the whim of his guards. A convict regarded as incorrigible would be sent to a penal settlement where conditions were so fearful that "the heart of a man who went to them was taken from him and he was given that of a beast." Norfolk Island, off New South Wales in the Pacific, and Port Arthur in Tasmania (then known as Van Diemen's Land) were two of the most notorious penal settlements.

Marcus Clarke's[1] novel *For the Term of his Natural Life* (1874) is the story of a convict in Australia. The opening chapters are set in 1827; the book ends with the death of its hero, Rufus Dawes, in 1846. We are shown the convict ship on its way to Australia, grossly overladen, the men crammed into cages between decks, savage, mutinous, dying of typhus. Rufus Dawes falls foul of the military commandant as soon as he arrives, is sent to work in a chain gang, and finally dispatched to the penal settlement of Port Arthur.

"He thrice attempted to escape, but escape was even more hopeless than it had been at Hell's Gates. The Peninsula of Port Arthur was admirably guarded, signal stations drew a chain round the prison, an armed boat's crew watched each bay, and across the narrow isthmus which connected it with the mainland was a cordon of watch-dogs, in addition to the soldier guard. He was retaken of course, flogged, and weighted with heavier irons. The second time, they sent him to the coal mines, where the prisoners lived underground, worked half naked, and dragged their inspecting

1 Marcus Clarke (1846–81). Emigrated to Australia in 1863. Wrote a number of plays and novels of which the above is best known.

gaolers in waggons upon iron tramways, when such great people con-
descended to visit them."

We are shown hideous floggings, torture at the whim of the administrator,
corruption and cruelty, and degradation so fearful that a small boy of
twelve jumps into the sea rather than endure more, and men agree to murder
each other in order that one may die and the other be hanged.

Marcus Clarke drew his material for this novel largely from the Report
of a Select Committee on Transportation printed in 1838. This Committee, after careful investigation, urged that transportation should cease,
and New South Wales itself was objecting so violently to the convicts
that the government was forced to take notice.

But if convicts could not be shipped overseas where could they be housed
at home? A compromise was made. The stream of convicts should be
directed only at Van Diemen's Land which had not so far protested, and
a new system of grading prisoners was introduced which it was hoped
would improve their lot. By this they could work themselves from grade
to grade upwards, and finish, if they were fortunate, as ticket-of-leave men
(that is, they were free, but answerable to the authorities), or – the top grade –
by being awarded unconditional freedom. But in practice the scheme broke
down; Van Diemen's Land became one vast prison settlement quite
unable to absorb the convicts into its population, and to the last the loath-
some conditions which Marcus Clarke had described persisted in Port
Arthur.

In England itself however there was strong reaction against the in-
humanities of the old criminal code, and in the 1830's and '40's there was
much done to soften this. But two relics of the old régime were to remain
for many years yet. There were the hulks and there was Newgate Gaol.

"There, at the very core of London, in the heart of its business and anima-
tion, in the midst of a whirl of noise and motion; stemming as it were the
giant currents of life that flow ceaselessly on from different quarters and meet
beneath its walls, stands Newgate," Dickens wrote in *Nicholas Nickleby*.

Newgate and the Bastille have probably stirred the imagination of
writers more than any other prisons in the world. Newgate had existed for
centuries. It was reserved for the worst class of prisoners, who until the 19th
century had been herded together regardless of sex, age, or their offence,
in conditions that were a byword for their overcrowding and filth. From

PRISONERS EXERCISING AT NEWGATE
Engraving by Doré (*London, 1872*)

1783 (when executions at Tyburn ceased), all London's public executions took place outside Newgate, a spectacle of enormous popularity for Londoners which was not finally abolished until 1868. Elizabeth Fry began her work of prison reform at Newgate in 1813, but though she brought some order there, radical reforms were not introduced until 1856, and only in 1881 did it cease to be used as a prison except for those awaiting trial at the Central Criminal Court. It was to stand at the heart of London, in the shadow of St. Paul's, for twenty years more, until it was finally demolished in 1902–3.

Standing grimly in the whirl of London life, it exerted a terrifying fascina-tion over the criminal and the law-abiding alike. It is one of the first buildings in London to be identified by Pip in *Great Expectations*, when he makes the momentous journey from his old home in Essex up to the great city where he is to be brought up as a gentleman. He sees the "great black dome of Saint Paul's bulging at me from behind a grim stone building which a bystander said was Newgate Prison." He deduces from the quantity of straw laid on the road to deaden the sound of traffic, and the quantity of people standing about smelling of drink, that the trials are on. "An exceedingly dirty and partially drunk minister of justice" offers to get him a place at the trials.

"As I declined the proposal on the plea of an appointment, he was so good as to take me into a yard and show me where the gallows was kept, and also where people were publicly whipped, and then he showed me the Debtors' Door, out of which culprits came to be hanged; heightening the interest of that dreadful portal by giving me to understand that 'four on 'em' would come out at that door the day after to-morrow at eight in the morning to be killed in a row."

The old unreformed Newgate of the 1830's dominates much of *Great Expectations*. The offices of the lawyer who disburses the convict's money to Pip lie only round the corner. They are frequented by the relations of criminals who seek Mr. Jaggers to defend them; they are decorated with the death masks of criminal clients of Mr. Jaggers who have been hanged at Newgate, and Mr. Jaggers has as a servant a murderess whom he has res-cued from the death penalty.

Dickens repeatedly referred to Newgate in his novels, and visited it more than once. He even witnessed a public execution there. He described 18th century Newgate in both his historical novels *Barnaby Rudge* and *The Tale of Two Cities*, and it is in the condemned cell of Newgate that Fagin spends his last hours and where Oliver Twist is led to visit him. Newgate held the same fascination for the criminals, who would throng to the public executions, discuss with ghoulish pleasure the fate of those behind its walls, and spell their way through the Newgate Calendar, a catalogue of the crimes of some of its most notorious inmates.

CONVICT HULKS
The Warrior, one of the Thames hulks.
Illustrated London News, 1846.

The hulks were an additional reminder of the old régime. Black relics of former naval men-of-war, they stood moored in the Thames and other rivers, condemned by all penal reformers. The idea of converting old ships into prisons arose when the American colonies were lost to England on the breaking out of the American War of Independence, and the government was left with no land overseas to receive its convicts. It was twenty years before Australia became available for the purpose and by that time the hulks had become so useful that it was hard to abandon them. As late as 1841 there were 3,552 convicts of the worst type on board the various hulks of England, in disgracefully overcrowded and squalid conditions. They were not finally abandoned until 1858.

Their most famous appearance in literature is in *Great Expectations*, written after they had ceased to be used. *Great Expectations* is the story of Pip, a young man dazzled by the idea of wealth, who complacently accepts anonymous gifts of money and the new social standing that this bestows on him, and then discovers that the unknown benefactor is in fact a convict.

He first meets this convict in the opening chapter of the book. Lingering in the churchyard near his home "in the marsh country, down by the river, within, as the river wound, twenty miles of the sea," he is terrified by "a fearful man, all in coarse grey, with a great iron on his leg," who seizes him and demands food and a file. Though Pip steals these for him, the convict is eventually recaptured. Pip is a witness of the scene, and watches the soldiers push the man into a rowing boat, rowed by a crew of convicts like himself.

"By the light of the torches, we saw the black hulk lying a little way from the mud of the shore, like a wicked Noah's ark. Cribbed and barred and moored by massive rusty chains, the prison-ship seemed in my young eyes to be ironed like the prisoners. We saw the boat go alongside, and we saw him taken up the side and disappear. Then the ends of the torches were flung hissing into the water, and went out, as if it were all over with him."

It is this convict who from thousands of miles away is to send back money to rear Pip as a gentleman, for it enchants him to think that he who has been in and out of prison all his life should hold the power of making a gentleman. "How strange it was that I should be encompassed by all this taint of prison and crime," Pip says to himself before he learns the source of his new fortune, as he reflects on his boyhood spent in the shadow of the hulks, and his new home in the shadow of Newgate. He is to learn by the end of the book that the taint has seeped into all the money that he has accepted so unthinkingly.

Though Victorian England found it hard to shake off these relics of an earlier age – Newgate, the hulks, and transportation – progress was made with the reform of prisons elsewhere. It was recognized that the old system of herding criminals together led to more crime than it prevented, and reformers agreed that a system of confinement in separate cells was to be desired. Opinions varied, however, on whether they should be isolated in separate cells with no contact with anybody but their custodians (the Separate System), or whether they should be housed in individual cells but allowed to mix with other prisoners under conditions of total silence (the Silent System).

The argument continued throughout the 19th century. In the '30's and '40's the Separate System was thought to be humane and likely to reform the prisoners who, the authorities hoped, would study the Bibles left in their cells and meditate on their sinful natures. By the 1860's it

THE "SILENT SYSTEM' AT PARKHURST PRISON

Elementary religious and moral instruction was given to young offenders at this prison, the boys carefully partitioned from each other to avoid contamination.
(*Illustrated London News*, 1847.)

was realized that the Separate System did not bring this about, and public opinion was reacting against the idealism of the early years of the reign. It was futile to try to alter prisoners' characters, it was held, and trust to the effect of religious teaching; what was needed was good hard punishment to deter men from crime.

Dickens in *David Copperfield* (1849–50) was concerned to show how those who tried to be charitable to prisoners could be deceived. David goes to visit Uriah Heep, that unctuous swindling hypocrite, now in prison for forgery and theft. He finds him comfortably housed (David and his creator, Dickens, are indignant at how comfortably housed and well-fed the prisoners are in this establishment) in a prison where the Separate System is in vogue. Uriah Heep is the admiration of all the authorities, a model prisoner, noted for his piety. He is reading a hymn book in his cell when David is shown in.

"'Well, Twenty Seven,' said Mr. Creakle, mournfully admiring him. 'How do you find yourself today?'

'I am so very umble, sir!' replied Uriah Heep.

'You are always so, Twenty Seven,' said Mr. Creakle.

Here, another gentleman asked, with extreme anxiety: 'Are you quite comfortable?'

'Yes, I thank you, sir!' said Uriah Heep, looking in that direction. 'Far more comfortable here, than ever I was outside. I see my follies now, sir. That's what makes me comfortable.'

Several gentlemen were much affected; and a third questioner, forcing himself to the front, inquired with extreme feeling: 'How do you find the beef?'

'Thank you, sir,' replied Uriah, glancing in the new direction of this voice, 'it was tougher yesterday than I could wish; but it's my duty to bear. I have committed follies, gentlemen,' said Uriah, looking round with a meek smile, 'and I ought to bear the consequences without repining.'"

The debate on how prisoners should be treated inevitably included what work they should be made to do. There were those who said they should be trained in some skill by which they could earn their living when they were freed. The harsher said no, they must be punished by performing some hard and useless labour which broke the spirit by

"TURN HIM OUT, RATCLIFF"

Throwing drunken sailors out from a beer-shop on to the Ratcliff Highway in
the London dock area.

Engraving by Doré (*London*, 1872).

its monotony and uselessness. To this end the treadmill and the crank were devised. The treadmill was a revolving cylinder with steps upon it. As the prisoners, each partitioned off from the next, trod up the steps so the wheel revolved. It was heavy, exhausting, much hated work, and was extensively used by prisons run on the Silent System, for the warders could see to it that the men did not speak to each other, and the partitions ensured that they did not communicate while they were on the wheel. Shot drill was another punishment that could be carried out in silence. Here the men had to stand endlessly shifting a pile of cannon balls from one side of them to the other and then back again. Crank labour, on the other hand, could be carried out in the isolation of the cell. A handle fixed in the wall had to be turned so many thousand times a day – again to no purpose whatever.

Charles Reade[1] in *It is Never too Late to Mend* (1856), written six years after *David Copperfield*, also protested about the Separate System. But whereas Dickens had made fun of the softness with which Uriah Heep and his companions were treated, Reade wrote with horror about the savage excesses that a cruel governor could introduce into such a system. He had in mind the recent scandal of Birmingham Prison and the abuses there for which the governor had actually been sentenced to imprisonment.

Good or bad, the systems the early Victorians devised for the punishment of crime were to remain in force for the rest of the century, and most of the present prison buildings have been inherited from them. A type of prison which has however totally disappeared and which the Victorians themselves took over from an earlier age was the debtors' prison. Imprisonment for debt was finally abolished in the 1860's. Debtors in London were usually sent to the Fleet, the King's Bench, or the Marshalsea prisons. Dickens wrote of all these; his father's imprisonment in the Marshalsea has already been described in chapter nine.

Dickens was by far the greatest of the novelists who wrote about crime. Few of his novels lack a thief, a swindler, or a murderer. He had the taste of the common man of his own day and of ours for crimes of violence, and he could readily understand the psychology of those that performed them. He was contemptuous of the romantic novel about

1 Charles Reade (1814–84). Author of plays and novels sometimes written for propaganda purposes. *The Cloister and the Hearth* is his best-known work.

THE MURDERER TRIES TO ESCAPE FROM HIS PURSUERS
George Cruikshank's illustration of the last moments of Bill Sikes, in *Oliver Twist*.

crime, such as Harrison Ainsworth and Lord Lytton[1] wrote in the early Victorian period. Novels of this sort, known as the "Newgate School" of writing, turned the criminal hero into a dashing, romantic figure, and completely distorted the true facts.

Reviewers who talked about the "Newgate School of Novelists" tended to include *Oliver Twist* among its products, to Dickens' profound indignation.

1 Edward Bulwer-Lytton (1803–73). His *Paul Clifford* and *Eugene Aram* are typical "Newgate School" novels.

"Take a small boy," said an early number of *Punch*, giving advice about how to cook up "a startling romance", and including therein all the ingredients of *Oliver Twist*, "charity, factory, carpenter's apprentice, or otherwise, as occasion may serve – stew him well down in vice – garnish largely with oaths and flash songs – boil him in a cauldron of crime and improbabilities. Season equally with good and bad qualities – infuse petty larceny, affection, benevolence, and burglary, honour and housebreaking, amiability and arson – boil all gently. Stew down a mad mother – a gang of robbers – several pistols – a bloody knife. Serve up with a couple of murders – and season with a hanging-match.

N.B. Alter the ingredients to a beadle and a workhouse – the scenes may be the same, but the whole flavour of vice will be lost, and the boy will turn out a perfect pattern. – Strongly recommended for weak stomachs."

Dickens reckoned that he had drawn his criminals in *Oliver Twist* with faithful reality "in all their deformity, in all their wretchedness, in all the squalid poverty of their lives; to show them as they really are, for ever skulking uneasily through the dirtiest paths of life, with the great, black, ghastly gallows closing up their prospect, turn them where they may."

Certainly Dickens, unlike Ainsworth, stripped the glamour from crime. He knew the Saffron Hill district where Fagin lived, its thieves' dens, stolen handkerchief trade, "flash" talk, its methods of training boy pickpockets, the way crime was organized there. But it is far from a sober, factual account of crime, for Dickens was excited and fascinated by the "deformity" of what he described, and "the great, black, ghastly gallows," and especially by crimes of violence, and the plot is as melo-dramatic as any of the Newgate School's.

Perhaps the most unlikely character is Oliver Twist himself. What child, given a workhouse upbringing such as Dickens described, with from birth no contact with anything but harshness and brutality and squalor, could grow into a mild and innocent boy, determined to stand out against wrong-doing and shuddering at the thought of theft? It is infinitely more likely that he would have turned into such a boy as Dicky Perrott, the child of the Jago.

Conclusion

THE danger about examining a particular period is that one may think of it as frozen in time, a fly embedded in amber, and so associate with it a certain appearance, a certain pattern of behaviour. Any period of time is continually changing, and none changed more than the Victorian scene which was so long and so varied that we have to refer to the early, the mid, and the late Victorian periods. To the early Victorians famine and revolution seemed to threaten the whole nation. To the late Victorians England seemed so secure that nothing could shake it. It is therefore more than usually misleading to try to attach any particular label to the people who lived in this reign.

One of the accusations commonly levelled at the Victorians is that they were complacent. It should now be obvious from the writings quoted in the preceding chapters that complacency is not a charge that can fairly be levelled at the thinking Victorians. They were keenly aware of the evils in their midst. They might not be able to suggest solutions for the problems but they exposed them, debated them, denounced them, in pamphlets, poems, sermons, novels, newspaper articles, books for children, in public and private enquiries. "There is not one question of home or foreign affairs," remarked Taine, "but it is dealt with very thoroughly in fifty newspaper articles, handled and examined from every point of view, and that with a power of reasoning and argument and a thoroughness of documentation that one cannot help admiring." In France, he said, the frankness with which the criticism was made would infallibly lead to duels and rioting; but in England the clamour in the press only resulted in meetings, protests, and petitions.

In England, said Taine, both evil and good are greater than elsewhere. This remark might especially be applied to the Victorian epoch.

Index